CONFERENCE PROCEEDINGS

Corporate Culture and Ethical Leadership Under the Federal Sentencing Guidelines

What Should Boards, Management, and Policymakers Do Now?

Michael D. Greenberg

 Center for Corporate Ethics and Governance

A RAND LAW, BUSINESS, AND REGULATION CENTER

This report was funded with pooled resources from the RAND Center for Corporate Ethics and Governance, a research center within RAND Law, Business, and Regulation, a division of the RAND Corporation.

Library of Congress Cataloging-in-Publication Data is available for this publication

ISBN: 978-08330-7695-3

The RAND Corporation is a nonprofit institution that helps improve policy and decisionmaking through research and analysis. RAND's publications do not necessarily reflect the opinions of its research clients and sponsors.

RAND® is a registered trademark.

Cover image courtesy of iStockphoto/Mark Herreid. Used with permission.

Published 2012 by the RAND Corporation
1776 Main Street, P.O. Box 2138, Santa Monica, CA 90407-2138
1200 South Hayes Street, Arlington, VA 22202-5050
4570 Fifth Avenue, Suite 600, Pittsburgh, PA 15213-2665
RAND URL: http://www.rand.org/
To order RAND documents or to obtain additional information, contact
Distribution Services: Telephone: (310) 451-7002;
Fax: (310) 451-6915; Email: order@rand.org

PREFACE

Since 1991, the Federal Sentencing Guidelines for Organizations have provided a criminal justice framework to deter and punish organizational misconduct. Over the years, amendments to the guidelines have expanded the scope of traditional compliance activities by reinforcing the notion of an organizational culture and by creating incentives for organizations to build cultures that "encourage ethical conduct and a commitment to compliance with the law." Interest in corporate culture and ethics has mounted in parallel to a push for new compliance regulation and more rigorous government oversight of the business sector. Meanwhile, a series of basic questions has emerged about how to build stronger ethical cultures within companies and the optimal role of government policy in this regard.

On May 16, 2012, the RAND Corporation convened a symposium in Washington, D.C., to address these and related questions. Invited participants included thought leaders from the ranks of public company directors and executives, ethics and compliance officers, and stakeholders from the government, academic, and nonprofit sectors.

These proceedings summarize key issues and topics from the symposium discussions. The document is not intended to be a transcript. Rather, it is organized by major theme and serves to highlight areas of agreement and disagreement among participants. With the exception of four invited papers that were written in advance and presented at the symposium, remarks are not attributed to individual participants.

Readers of these proceedings may also be interested in the following RAND documents:

- *For Whom the Whistle Blows: Advancing Corporate Compliance and Integrity Efforts in the Era of Dodd-Frank*, CF-290-CCEG, 2011, http://www.rand.org/pubs/conf_proceedings/CF290.html
- *Directors as Guardians of Compliance and Ethics Within the Corporate Citadel: What the Policy Community Should Know*, CF-277-CCEG, 2010, http://www.rand.org/pubs/conf_proceedings/CF277.html
- *Perspectives of Chief Ethics and Compliance Officers on the Detection and Prevention of Corporate Misdeeds: What the Policy Community Should Know*, CF-258-RC, 2009, http://www.rand.org/pubs/conf_proceedings/CF258.html.

THE RAND CENTER FOR CORPORATE ETHICS AND GOVERNANCE

The RAND Center for Corporate Ethics and Governance, a research center within RAND Law, Business, and Regulation (LBR), is committed to improving public understanding of corporate ethics, law, and governance and to identifying specific ways in which businesses can operate ethically, legally, and profitably. The center's work is supported by voluntary contributions from private-sector organizations and individuals with interests in research on these topics.

LBR, a research division of the RAND Corporation, is dedicated to improving policy and decisionmaking in civil justice, corporate ethics and governance, and business regulation. It serves policymakers and executives in both government and the private sector through studies of controversial and challenging issues in these areas. Its work builds on a long tradition of RAND research characterized by an interdisciplinary, empirical approach to public policy issues and rigorous standards of quality, objectivity, and independence.

LBR research is supported by pooled grants from a range of sources, including corporations, trade and professional associations, individuals, government agencies, and private foundations. It disseminates its work widely to policymakers, practitioners in law and business, other researchers, and the public. In accordance with RAND policy, all its reports are subject to peer review. Its publications do not necessarily reflect the opinions or policies of its research sponsors.

For more information on LBR, see http://lbr.rand.org or contact the director:

Paul Heaton
Acting Director, RAND Law, Business, and Regulation
1776 Main Street
P.O. Box 2138
Santa Monica, CA 90407-2138
310-393-0411 x7526
Paul_Heaton@rand.org

For more information on the RAND Center for Corporate Ethics and Governance, see http://lbr.rand.org/cceg or contact the director:

Michael Greenberg
Director, RAND Center for Corporate Ethics and Governance
4570 Fifth Avenue, Suite 600
Pittsburgh, PA 15213
412-683-2300 x4648
Michael_Greenberg@rand.org

CONTENTS

SUMMARY

In 1991, the U.S. Sentencing Commission (USSC) expanded the Federal Sentencing Guidelines to provide a consistent set of penalties to deter and justly punish organizational crime. The sentencing structure was also intended to encourage positive behavior—specifically, the establishment of effective compliance programs within firms. In principle, such programs offer a primary internal line of defense for corporations in detecting and preventing corporate and workplace misconduct that might otherwise lead to criminal prosecution.

In the two decades since 1991, there have been multiple amendments to the Federal Sentencing Guidelines for Organizations (FSGO). One of the most notable was a 2004 addition that set out a corporate obligation "to promote an organizational culture that encourages ethical behavior and compliance with law." Ultimately, one of the chief aims of the FSGO has been to encourage basic cultural change within organizations, with the goal of reducing both criminal and ethical risk.

This focus on organizational culture as an antecedent to misbehavior highlights a subtle but important thread in compliance and ethics (C&E) practice. A narrow view of compliance within corporations can too easily focus on simply parsing and following the law, including implementing controls to ensure that relevant laws are understood and obeyed. Critics have described this as a "check-the-box" approach, cautioning that it does not address the fundamental drivers of organizational behavior and that it can contribute to a false sense of security. By contrast, an emphasis on corporate culture goes well beyond the technical exercise of interpreting and following legal rules. The aim is to foster a fundamental understanding of the collective behavior and values of the people who make up the corporation and to ensure that they are aligned with the corporation's ideals of honesty and fair dealing. In this way, the corporate culture becomes broadly preventative of misconduct and violations of the law.

For chief ethics and compliance officers (CECOs), corporate board members, and C-suite executives, the emphasis on culture in the FSGO raises a set of challenging operational questions. For example, how can management intervene to modify organizational culture, and what are the various roles and responsibilities of senior executives and directors in this regard? The questions differ somewhat for policymakers: When the guidelines identify the pursuit of an ethical culture as one criterion for an effective C&E program, what exactly does that mean? And how far can the USSC and policymakers usefully go in using law enforcement and regulation to promote corporate intangibles, such as culture and ethics in the workplace?

It was in this context that RAND convened the May 16, 2012, symposium "Corporate Culture and Ethical Leadership Under the Federal Sentencing Guidelines: What Should Boards, Management, and Policymakers Do Now?" The objective was to stimulate a broad conversation about organizational culture following the 20th anniversary of the FSGO, as well as to explore the business and policy ramifications of efforts to build better ethical cultures in corporations. The symposium also built on previous RAND-hosted roundtable meetings that focused on the roles of corporate boards, CECOs, and internal whistleblower mechanisms in helping firms address C&E challenges. The May 2012 symposium brought together a group of two dozen senior thought leaders from the ranks of public company directors and executives, CECOs, and stakeholders from the government, academic, and nonprofit sectors. Discussions focused on practical steps that can be taken to strengthen corporate ethical culture and the unique roles of directors, CECOs, top executives, and government policy in pursuing that end.

Several major themes emerged from these discussions. First, the FSGO focus on corporate ethical culture reflects a policy goal to cultivate shared values, behavior, and collective responsibility within organizations rather than simply encouraging compliance with the law as a purely technical and procedural exercise. Second, there are different ways to interpret "corporate ethical culture," and firms must overcome or sidestep problems in moral philosophy that might otherwise paralyze practical C&E efforts. For example, one way to make a firm's ethical culture more concrete is by focusing on employee behaviors and other factors that tend to interfere with employee perceptions of commitment, integrity, and transparency in the corporate workplace. Overcoming these barriers offers an avenue for a firm to align its values with workplace behaviors and to energize protective behaviors on the part of both employees and management. A third broad symposium theme highlighted the various practical steps that C&E programs, senior executives, corporate boards, and policymakers can take to contribute to stronger ethical cultures within corporations. Prominent among these is the simple recognition that ethical culture is, in fact, an important priority, that a strong ethical culture is desirable both intrinsically and for its value in limiting reputational risk and cultivating shareholder trust, and that efforts to build a stronger ethical culture may be closely linked to both effective C&E programs and stronger and more empowered CECOs.

INVITED REMARKS FROM FIVE PANELISTS

The initial session of the symposium was dedicated to remarks from five panelists who represented expert viewpoints on compliance law, corporate ethical culture consulting, and the C&E function within firms. Their remarks were based on invited white papers distributed in advance of the symposium. The white papers, listed here, are reproduced in Appendix C of these proceedings.

- Jeffrey M. Kaplan, a partner at the law firm Kaplan & Walker LLP, "Semi-Tough: A Short History of Compliance and Ethics Program Law"
- David Gebler, president of Skout Group, LLC, a corporate consultancy, "The Start of the Slippery Slope: Why Leaders Must Manage Culture to Create a Sustainable Ethics and Compliance Program"
- Patrick Gnazzo, principal of Better Business Practices LLC, and Keith Darcy, executive director of the Ethics and Compliance Officer Association, "Preventing Corporate Crime: What Boards and Management Should Do Next to Support Ethical Culture and Stronger C&E Programs"

- Joseph Murphy, director of public policy at the Society for Corporate Compliance and Ethics, "Over 20 Years Since the Federal Sentencing Guidelines: What Government Can Do Next to Support Effective Compliance and Ethics Programs."

HOW MUCH PROGRESS HAVE COMPANIES MADE IN MEETING THE CULTURAL GOALS SET OUT BY THE FEDERAL SENTENCING GUIDELINES FOR ORGANIZATIONS?

The second session of the symposium featured a moderated discussion addressing a series of basic questions about the nature and extent of corporate progress in fulfilling the ethical culture mandates in the FSGO. The session opened with some observations about the importance of ethical culture as an adjunct to a corporation's formal compliance efforts. Participants noted that there is no simple set of controls that can fully prevent rule-breaking in a large organization and that "culture" represents a shared commitment to good behavior that goes beyond the technical exercise of simply parsing and obeying the law. It was also observed that every employee in the corporation, "from the shipping clerk to the lead director," has a role to play in contributing to this kind of culture. One participant cited an example in which an executive secretary received an anonymous package of stolen trade secrets from a corporate competitor and immediately took it to the general counsel—without reading the contents or passing the package to her own supervisor. The participant stated that this was both the right thing to do and a decision that helped safeguard the company from potentially significant exposure during the subsequent outside investigation. It also reflected the influence of a strong culture and shared ethical commitment within that company. A question was then posed: How can corporate leaders go about cultivating these sorts of shared values and commitments within their own organizations?

Participants in the session expressed a range of opinions about the extent to which the FSGO had been successful in prompting real improvements in corporate cultures. Some argued that considerable progress had been made by companies in meeting specific compliance program standards under the FSGO and that this progress, together with the new focus on culture, has had a positive (though difficult to quantify) impact on the field. Others expressed more mixed views. One observed that high-profile corporate efforts to suppress and punish internal whistleblowers continue to abound despite the FSGO, adding that such actions run counter to efforts to develop stronger ethical cultures. Another participant suggested that many chief executive officers and boards continue to prioritize short-term performance, a move that often fails to accommodate initiatives to foster stronger cultures. In such cases, related structural problems in governance and performance incentives can undermine the impact of the FSGO. Still other participants observed that it is difficult even to analyze a specific corporation's "culture," and, consequently, the influence of the FSGO in contributing to more ethical environments is difficult to quantify. Several participants also noted that an indeterminate but significant number of firms have fallen short of implementing rigorous compliance programs based on FSGO standards. In turn, such firms are unlikely to have experienced much of an impact on their cultures as a result of the FSGO.

The symposium discussion generated several points of agreement among participants:

- Effective C&E programs and strong organizational cultures are deeply connected.
- In some important and practical ways, corporate ethical culture can be measured.
- Corporate boards have a central role to play in building stronger ethical cultures.
- Top executives also have a key role in building stronger ethical cultures.
- Culture is the "missing link" that drives employee behavior, including the decisions of internal whistleblowers to come forward or stay silent.

WHAT ARE THE BARRIERS TO ACHIEVING STRONGER ETHICAL CULTURES AND MORE EFFECTIVE C&E PROGRAMS IN FIRMS, AND WHAT SHOULD BOARDS, MANAGEMENT, AND POLICYMAKERS DO NEXT?

Participants in the final session of the symposium engaged in a more in-depth discussion on improving ethical culture and C&E efforts within firms, identifying tangible next steps to those ends. The session opened with some reflections on the high-profile breakdown of the ethical culture at WorldCom more than a decade ago, which ultimately led to the collapse of that company. Participants noted that the deficiencies at WorldCom did not stem from an isolated accounting problem or single rogue executive but, rather, a more entrenched set of shortcomings that involved multiple gatekeepers and executives who did not carry out their responsibilities. Other contributing factors included a lack of transparency and information-sharing between senior management and the board, the corrosive influence of excessive greed among some top executives, and a collective failure to carry out the company's fiduciary duty to shareholders. The problems at WorldCom were described as "cultural" (in the sense that they were deep and widespread), reflecting a lack of "tone at the top," and perverting controls and corporate governance mechanisms that, on paper, should have helped to prevent the breakdown. The discussion touched on the policy response to the company's collapse as well: The subsequent Sarbanes-Oxley (SOX) legislation included multiple provisions designed to address specific problems that were revealed by the scandals at WorldCom. Without commenting directly on the success of SOX, participants suggested that progress in addressing the deeper cultural challenges illustrated by WorldCom's failure would likely require a new and different type of commitment from boards and management.

Much of the discussion addressed how to facilitate this kind of cultural change within corporations and how to overcome existing corporate barriers. Some participants questioned how law and policy might be used to try to promote these ends and whether it would be appropriate to expand or refine the FSGO. Other strands of the discussion focused more on specific actions that boards and senior management could take to foster stronger cultures within their organizations. It was noted that a significant part of the challenge lies simply in convincing top executives and boards to *want* to advocate for stronger ethical cultures. Participants agreed that the ties between a deficient ethical culture and lapses in compliance, and between lapses in compliance and reputational risk, are an important part of the calculus in making the case for stronger C&E programs to executives and boards. Participants also observed that a central challenge involves overcoming the perception among executives, boards, and policymakers that ethical culture and behavior are either easy or prohibitively difficult, to cultivate within an organization. In the end, the discussion emphasized the need to identify some concrete steps to overcome both forms of inertia. One participant noted that corporate boards and executives too often believe that "tone at the top" is about talk rather than action and lack insight into specific interventions that might support better culture: "If you are not managing culture, then culture is managing you."

The session's discussion highlighted the following areas of agreement among participants:

- An independent, empowered CECO is a key ingredient in achieving a stronger ethical culture.
- Performance incentives offer a critical tool for driving ethical culture as a priority within organizations.
- Companies need to commit to periodic self-assessments of ethical culture as a part of their C&E programs.
- Policymakers should reward companies for implementing superior C&E programs and cultures while punishing deficiencies.
- Boards and executives need to grapple with the value proposition for a strong ethical culture.
- Firms need to overcome a legalistic, check-the-box view of compliance.

ACKNOWLEDGMENTS

I wish to thank the panelists, speakers, and all those who participated in the roundtable discussions, without whom the exchange of ideas documented here would not have been possible. I would particularly like to thank the invited white paper authors who spoke at the symposium: Jeffrey M. Kaplan, David Gebler, Patrick Gnazzo, Keith Darcy, and Joseph Murphy. Dick Thornburgh and Larry Thompson also made notable contributions to the conversation, as did Stephen Cohen, Carlo di Florio, and John Steer. A full list of participants and their affiliations can be found in Appendix B. My symposium co-chair, Donna Boehme, provided invaluable contributions in structuring and facilitating the discussions and in helping to bring the right group of people to the conference table.

Finally, I would also like to thank Jamie Morikawa, Stephanie Shedd, Katie Allen, and Sarah Hauer at RAND for their assistance in organizing the symposium, managing logistics, capturing the discussions on the day of the event, and generating these proceedings.

ABBREVIATIONS

C&E	compliance and ethics
CECO	chief ethics and compliance officer
CEO	chief executive officer
FCPA	Foreign Corrupt Practices Act
FSGO	Federal Sentencing Guidelines for Organizations
LBR	RAND Law, Business, and Regulation
SOX	Sarbanes-Oxley Act of 2002
USSC	U.S. Sentencing Commission

1. INTRODUCTION

In today's complex corporate environment, far-flung operations and multijurisdictional transactions are often the norm, but companies still depend on their individual managers, employees, and agents to do business. Instances of misconduct and law-breaking on the part of employees and executives have the potential to generate serious negative consequences for firms, not only through reputational and economic harm but also through direct criminal and civil liability for the wrongdoing. In 1991, in recognition that the acts of individuals can create criminal liability for their organizations, the U.S. Sentencing Commission (USSC) expanded the Federal Sentencing Guidelines to include a new chapter on organizational crime. The intent of Chapter 8 was to provide a consistent set of guidelines to deter and justly punish organizational crime. The sentencing structure was also intended to encourage positive behavior—specifically, the establishment of effective compliance programs within firms. In principle, such programs offer a primary internal line of defense for corporations in detecting and preventing corporate and workplace misconduct that might otherwise lead to criminal prosecution.

In the two decades since 1991, there have been multiple amendments to the original Chapter 8 Federal Sentencing Guidelines for Organizations (FSGO). Explicit standards were added to define the elements of an effective compliance program, to stress the responsibility of corporate boards to "be knowledgeable" and to exercise "reasonable oversight" of the company's compliance activities, and to highlight the role of chief ethics and compliance officers (CECOs) in the day-to-day management of compliance programs. By establishing these detailed parameters, the USSC helped to both codify the requirements for effective compliance and create a set of leniency incentives for organizations implementing their own compliance activities. One of the most important amendments to the guidelines sets out a corporate obligation "to promote an organizational culture that encourages ethical behavior and compliance with law." Ultimately, one of the chief aims of the FSGO has been to encourage basic cultural change within organizations in ways that might reduce both criminal and ethical risk.

This focus on organizational culture as an antecedent to misbehavior highlights a subtle but important thread in compliance and ethics (C&E) practice. A narrow view of compliance by corporations can too easily focus on simply parsing and following the law, including implementing controls to ensure that relevant laws are understood and obeyed. By contrast, an emphasis on the corporate compliance culture goes well beyond the technical exercise of interpreting and following legal rules. The aim is to foster a fundamental understanding of the collective behavior and values of the people who make up the corporation and to ensure that they are aligned with the corporation's ideals of honesty and fair dealing. In this way, the corporate culture becomes broadly preventative of misconduct and violations of the law.

For CECOs, corporate board members, and C-suite executives, the organizational culture emphasis in the FSGO raises a set of challenging operational questions. For example, how can management intervene to modify organizational culture, and what are the various roles and responsibilities of senior executives and directors in this regard? The questions differ somewhat for policymakers: When the guidelines identify the pursuit of an ethical culture as one criterion for an effective C&E program, what exactly does that mean? And how far can the USSC and policymakers usefully go in using law enforcement and regulation to promote corporate intangibles, such as culture and ethics in the workplace?

The discussion of organizational culture as a priority for management comes at a time when both the C&E profession and the business community as a whole are engaged in an active process of self-assessment. Prominent commentators in the C&E field have observed that too many corporations have relegated their compliance programs to a "check-the-box" activity, designed to meet superficial legal requirements but lacking the substance to truly protect their organizations against wrongdoing. Put another way, 20 years after the introduction of the FSGO, corporate compliance efforts in some quarters have arguably stalled. The business community, meanwhile, has been struggling to address a broader loss of trust in business institutions in the aftermath of scandals and the financial crisis. Recent publications by the Conference Board, the National Association of Corporate Directors, and the Committee for Economic Development have all suggested the need for new board-level fiduciary responsibilities for C&E and risk management as a way to begin to address the perceived crisis in public confidence. When combined with the empirical observation that corporate workplace misconduct remains widespread, these developments suggest that C&E policy and practices currently stand at a crossroads. Organizational culture is potentially a missing link that could help propel a stronger set of C&E efforts—and more effective corporate prevention and self-policing practices—in the future.

It was in this context that RAND convened the May 16, 2012, symposium "Corporate Culture and Ethical Leadership Under the Federal Sentencing Guidelines: What Should Boards, Management, and Policymakers Do Now?" The objective was to stimulate a broad conversation about organizational culture following the 20th anniversary of the FSGO, as well as to explore the business and policy ramifications of efforts to build better ethical cultures in corporations. The symposium also built on previous RAND-hosted roundtable meetings that focused on the roles of corporate boards, CECOs, and internal whistleblower mechanisms in helping firms address C&E challenges.[1] The May 2012 symposium brought together a group of two dozen

---

[1] See Michael D. Greenberg, *For Whom the Whistle Blows: Advancing Corporate Compliance and Integrity Efforts in the Era of Dodd-Frank*, Santa Monica, Calif.: RAND Corporation, CF-290-CCEG, 2011, http://www.rand.org/pubs/conf_proceedings/CF290.html; Michael D. Greenberg, *Directors as Guardians of Compliance and Ethics Within the Corporate Citadel: What the Policy Community Should Know*, Santa Monica, Calif.: RAND Corporation, CF-277-CCEG, 2010, http://www.rand.org/pubs/conf_proceedings/CF277.html; and Michael D. Greenberg, *Perspectives of Chief Ethics and Compliance Officers on the Detection and Prevention of Corporate Misdeeds: What the Policy Community Should Know*, Santa Monica, Calif.: RAND Corporation, CF-258-RC, 2009, http://www.rand.org/pubs/conf_proceedings/CF258.html.

senior thought leaders from the ranks of public company directors and executives, CECOs, and stakeholders from the government, academic, and nonprofit sectors. Discussions focused on practical steps that can be taken to strengthen corporate ethical culture and the unique roles of directors, top executives, CECOs, and government policy in pursuing that end. The symposium agenda can be found in Appendix A of these proceedings, and the full list of participants is provided in Appendix B.

Prior to the symposium, several of the invited participants were asked to prepare and present formal remarks on corporate culture and the 20th anniversary of the FSGO. Their papers, distributed in advance of the event, represented the varied perspectives of outside counsel, corporate culture consulting, and CECOs. The speakers presented their remarks during the first session of the symposium; Chapter Two of these proceedings features short summaries of these remarks, and Appendix C presents the full text of the invited papers.

The second session of the symposium involved a moderated discussion on the topic of how much progress companies have made in meeting the cultural goals outlined in the FSGO. Chapter Three summarizes the major themes and topics of conversation in the session.

The third and final session of the symposium involved a moderated discussion of the barriers to achieving a stronger ethical culture and what corporate boards, management, and policymakers can do to facilitate such a culture and implement stronger C&E programs. Chapter Four summarizes the major themes and ideas from that session.

2. INVITED REMARKS FROM SYMPOSIUM PARTICIPANTS

OVERVIEW

The symposium began with remarks from five of the participants in attendance: Jeffrey M. Kaplan, a partner at the law firm Kaplan & Walker LLP; David Gebler, president of Skout Group, LLC, a corporate consultancy; Patrick Gnazzo, principal of Better Business Practices LLC; Keith Darcy, executive director of the Ethics and Compliance Officer Association; and Joseph Murphy, director of public policy at the Society for Corporate Compliance and Ethics. Their remarks were based on invited white papers, which are reproduced in Appendix C of these proceedings. Each author and topic brought an important expert viewpoint and set the context for the symposium discussions. This chapter presents brief summaries of each set of remarks.

SUMMARY:
SEMI-TOUGH: A SHORT HISTORY OF COMPLIANCE AND ETHICS PROGRAM LAW

Jeffrey M. Kaplan, Kaplan & Walker LLP

The Federal Sentencing Guidelines for Organizations

There is no one origin for laws related to corporate C&E programs, but the advent of the FSGO in 1991 was surely a seminal event. The FSGO helped the U.S. government pioneer the use of legal incentives for companies to develop C&E programs. Its twofold approach consists of the threat of harsh criminal penalties for violations and the prospect of leniency for firms that make a sincere effort to establish effective programs. The FSGO not only created new incentives for C&E programs, but it also provided a broad outline for what such programs should look like: the now epochal "seven steps" (i.e., implementation of standards; high-level oversight; due care in delegation, training, auditing, and internal reporting; enforcement; and appropriate responses to problems found). These steps are intuitive as a matter of sound risk management, but the FSGO elevated them to something akin to the force of law.

The 1990s

Corporate C&E programs became far more prevalent in the 1990s, in large part because of the influence of the FSGO. Membership in the Ethics Officer Association (formed in 1992) rose from 12 initial members to 632 members by the year 2000. Meanwhile, several high-profile corporate cases prosecuted under the FSGO resulted in hundreds of millions of dollars in fines against such companies as Archer Daniels Midland, Daiwa Bank, and Hoffman-La Roche, thereby escalating the stakes and strengthening the business case for corporate C&E programs. Other supporting developments included U.S. Department of Justice prosecutorial guidance, several key U.S. Supreme Court decisions, and a ruling by the Delaware Court of Chancery, all of which helped to reinforce the role of C&E programs in protecting against risk.

The Golden Age: 2001–2004

The most important developments in C&E law occurred during this four-year window, in the wake of the high-profile scandals at Enron and WorldCom. Notable among them were the passage of Sarbanes-Oxley, which included several new C&E mandates; the adoption of new corporate governance listing requirements by the New York Stock Exchange and NASDAQ, which also included C&E mandates; and the publication of highly detailed C&E program guidance for pharmaceutical manufacturers by the Office of the Inspector General in the U.S. Department of Health and Human Services. Most important in shaping C&E program expectations were the 2004 revisions to the FSGO, which defined an "effective C&E program" in far more detailed and rigorous terms. The revisions also included new guidelines that outlined the C&E responsibilities of corporate boards and senior management, specified that internal incentives should be part of a C&E program, and emphasized organizational "culture" as a defining element for an effective C&E program.

Recent Developments in C&E Law: An Age of Ambiguity

The most recent several years are harder to summarize, as there has been both forward and backward movement in C&E program law. The 2008 financial meltdown underscored the importance of organizational incentives and culture in mitigating compliance risk in large corporations. And the subsequent Dodd-Frank Act of 2010 instituted new whistleblower rules, again enhancing the business case for strong C&E programs.

The 2010 FSGO revisions enhanced independence-related expectations for C&E officers. Such expectations were also reinforced in various settlements (deferred prosecution or non-prosecution agreements) that set forth C&E program expectations for the defendant organizations.

In the anticorruption realm, large fines in Foreign Corrupt Practices Act (FCPA) litigation, fraud and abuse in the pharmaceuticals industry, and antitrust cases have underscored the importance of the FSGO in enforcement decisions (and, by extension, the incentive for strong C&E programs). There has also been an unprecedented global expansion of C&E programs, particularly in connection with anti-bribery standards issued by the Organisation for Economic Co-operation and Development in 2009 and the passage of the UK Bribery Act of 2010 (together with subsequent UK compliance guidance).

Despite all this activity, anecdotal evidence from recent years nevertheless suggests that many companies have cut back on their commitment to C&E programs, perhaps because there has been little indication that effective C&E programs really do matter in enforcement decisions. In 2012, the corporate community is increasingly divided into high-performing C&E "haves" and low-performing C&E "have-nots."

What Lies Ahead?

It is difficult to forecast what the future of C&E law will look like. On the one hand, an optimistic vision would include more consistent enforcement activity, better government communication about the benefits of strong C&E programs, further expansion of the incentives for independent C&E officers and ethical culture, and the evolution of laws and standards from other countries in a manner that parallels U.S. developments. On the other hand, there is the possibility that C&E may be sacrificed by the government to the cause of business necessity, or "hollowed out" through absorption into the general area of risk management.

SUMMARY:
THE START OF THE SLIPPERY SLOPE: HOW LEADERS CAN MANAGE CULTURE TO CREATE A SUSTAINABLE ETHICS AND COMPLIANCE PROGRAM

David Gebler, Skout Group, LLC

Putting Culture First

Most organizational leaders now subscribe to the concept that "culture trumps compliance," but what does that really mean? Ethical culture does not follow automatically from the seven steps of the FSGO, nor can corporate cultural change be achieved by working through a simple checklist of soft-skill requirements. In fact, the culture within an organization is determined primarily by what people actually do rather than what they *should* do. Thus, culture has more to do with real-world behavior and the work environment than with prescriptive rules. Although leaders can influence culture, for better or worse, they cannot mandate it. Culture is the social framework within which any C&E program must operate. Get the culture wrong and nothing else is likely to matter.

Elements of Culture

There are three core elements that define culture: the organization's mission and goals (the "what"), its principles and beliefs (the "why"), and its formal and informal standards of behavior (the "how"). Every organization has these elements, and employees can sense—even if they cannot articulate the specifics—whether there is internal consistency and whether they work together coherently or in conflict with one another within in the organization. When the three elements of culture are out of alignment, maladaptive employee and organizational behaviors tend to manifest.

Culture and Behavior

It is particularly important to recognize that culture and prevailing social norms can have a tremendous influence on the behavior of individuals. People tend to act in a way that is consistent with the norms established by their peers and leaders. Where organizational values and culture are not clearly stated, employees will look for cues for how to behave. The research of social psychologists dating back to Kurt Lewin in the 1930s has shown that social norms and cues can often be surprisingly powerful in determining behavior, including ethical behavior. Where organizational culture and norms fail to send the right signals, even honest and conscientious employees can become vulnerable to self-deception, rationalization, and disengagement.

A New Way of Thinking

The biggest challenge in managing an ethical culture in an organization involves the early detection of risk—that is, prior to the manifestation of overt compliance problems (e.g., criminal misbehavior, wildly opportunistic risk-taking). Under pressure to meet aggressive operational goals, many leaders find themselves adhering to the strategy of "If it ain't broke, don't fix it." In successful ethical cultures, by contrast, leaders tend to be alert to early warning signals. An important way to facilitate risk sensitivity and preventive action among leaders is to make the early warning signals, and potential corrective steps, as concrete as possible.

Getting to the Start of the Slippery Slope

To change ethical behavior and norms in an organization, leaders need to address major points of misalignment in the culture, particularly the ways in which organizational goals, principles, and standards come into conflict with each other.

There are several basic types of intervention that can be very effective in addressing such problems. *Accountability interventions* seek to boost organizational integrity by harmonizing goals (what the organization strives to do) with standards of behavior (how things are actually done). In parallel, accountability involves ensuring that both leaders and employees are "walking the talk" and are held accountable for their actions. By extension, accountability implies consistency, predictability, and fairness in organizational processes.

Incentive interventions seek to boost organizational commitment by linking organizational principles to goals and helping employees bring their own ethical principles to support their work. When principles and organizational goals are well aligned, employees tend to feel a stronger connection, commitment, and level of engagement with the firm. Organizational incentive structures can and should be designed to maximize that alignment and to reward employee behavior that reflects the best principles, as well as the goals, of the organization.

Transparency interventions seek to boost the alignment of an organization's standards— how things are done—with its principles and basic values. Where the standards are consistent with principles, there tends to be clarity in how the organization operates. One hallmark of this kind of clarity involves ensuring that employees feel safe to ask questions and raise concerns. That kind of transparency and engagement is one of the most visible and effective contributors to an ethical corporate culture.

Making It Happen

Consistent ethical leadership does not happen on its own. Specific targets for cultural intervention and related performance metrics and incentives can help corporate leaders move their firms in the right direction. And boards and CECOs both have critical roles to play: the former in holding senior management accountable for actively managing culture and the latter in independently "speaking truth to power" and advising leadership on the "soft stuff" that sits at the top of the cultural slippery slope.

SUMMARY:
PREVENTING CORPORATE CRIME: WHAT BOARDS AND MANAGEMENT SHOULD DO TO SUPPORT ETHICAL CULTURE AND STRONGER COMPLIANCE PROGRAMS

Patrick Gnazzo, Better Business Practices, LLC
Keith Darcy, Ethics and Compliance Officer Association

Despite two decades of investment in C&E programs since the birth of the FSGO, there continue to be gaps in companies' efforts to "prevent and detect" corporate crime and misconduct and in their overall ethical cultures. But what can boards and management do to take C&E programs, and the ethical culture that sustains them, to the next level of effectiveness?

The Board Must Oversee Corporate Culture

Analysts and commentators almost always focus on the chief executive officer (CEO) and the senior management team as the drivers of the organizational "tone at the top" but overlook the equally critical role of the board. However, many experts believe that the role of the board is at least as important, if not more so.

Why should the board be viewed as the primary sentinel for ethical culture in an organization? Senior executives, including the CEO, change frequently during the life of an organization. If management sets the culture, then the culture may become a moving target. Board members, meanwhile, tend to have longer tenure. The board is both well positioned and has a fiduciary responsibility to ensure that the organization's ethical culture does not erode when CEOs (and executive priorities) change. That responsibility has become more salient in recent years as concerns about reputation risk have tied ethical culture more directly to shareholder value.

Board oversight for a culture of integrity includes responsibility for undertaking serious conversations with management about such topics as quality, safety, honesty, environmental stewardship, and philanthropy. Board oversight also demands building explicit incentives into compensation and evaluation for executives and managers throughout the organization to reward integrity and other key cultural norms and objectives. And it requires the appointment of an empowered, adequately resourced, and independent CECO, who leads the C&E effort, to help drive ethical culture and to report back to the board with unfiltered access. There are many concrete steps that a board can take to strengthen and safeguard an organization's ethical culture.

The CEO and Senior Management Are the Drivers of Corporate Culture

Only when a CEO and senior leadership view ethical culture as an important part of their responsibilities and not merely as the CECO's delegated task will an ethical culture be created. Absent consistent commitment and modeling of desired behavior by top executives, it is all too easy for a "slippery slope" to develop, in which ethical conduct is not widely valued or practiced.

But just as history has disproved the old argument that a code of conduct is not needed because "we only hire good people," the notion that corporate leaders will instinctively and consistently know how to drive ethical leadership is similarly unreasonable. This is why the role of the CECO is so important. It is part of the CECO's mandate to create systems that help drive ethical culture, to detect and prevent misconduct, and to facilitate and support leadership to these ends. Together, the CEO and the board can ensure that there is a strong mandate for an empowered and independent CECO. Here, again, the CECO is a linchpin and central resource for the CEO and senior executive team, as well as for the board.

There are countless ways that the CEO and management can work together to embed ethical culture into the operations of the organization and to support an effective C&E program. Some illustrative examples include acting as models, in words and action, in support of the organizational code of conduct; modeling high standards of behavior in business decisions and strategy; participating visibly in C&E training and related processes; and insisting on the toughest discipline when a member of the top brass breaks the company's rules or threatens retaliation.

Conclusion

For companies to progress to the next step in their efforts to embed an ethical culture and to detect and prevent misconduct, both the board and senior management must take on more proactive roles. The CECO stands ready to develop, lead, and oversee C&E activities, as well as to advise both the board and senior management. But only with true engagement and consistent support from the board and the C-suite will the private sector reach that elusive next level of effectiveness and truly achieve the self-governance and the ethical culture goals envisioned by the FSGO.

SUMMARY:
OVER 20 YEARS SINCE THE FEDERAL SENTENCING GUIDELINES: WHAT GOVERNMENT CAN DO NEXT TO SUPPORT EFFECTIVE COMPLIANCE AND ETHICS PROGRAMS

Joseph Murphy, Society of Corporate Compliance and Ethics

Strong C&E programs do not spontaneously emerge from the corporate world. Rather, government has consistently been a catalyst for them. The FSGO are the best example of this relationship. Going forward, what steps can government take to amplify and facilitate stronger C&E efforts within companies?

Start with a Strong, Consistent Policy

The FSGO approach to recognizing and promoting effective corporate self-policing is strong but limited. Weak and inconsistent policies elsewhere in government undercut recognition of the importance of C&E programs and their role in performing an essential public service. Consequently, what is most needed from government is a strong, consistent policy in support of robust C&E practices. Formal cabinet-level and legislative endorsement of C&E programs is desirable as a next step. Congress, in particular, should recognize the power of prevention, and by extension, the social value of companies that are engaged in self-policing. This should be articulated as an important public policy goal, and one to be considered by regulators when issuing rules, enforcement agencies when pursuing violations, and courts in applying the law.

Tie the Policy to Enforcement Decisions in a Meaningful Way

To bring the policy to life, it is essential that enforcement agencies take C&E programs into account in their decisionmaking. These agencies can then make a more informed assessment about (1) whether to proceed against a company at all, (2) whether to prosecute criminally or civilly, (3) what charges to bring, (4) how much of a penalty to pursue, (5) whether to charge individuals rather than the company, (6) whether to pursue a subsidiary instead of a parent company, and (7) whether and to what extent to seek additional relief (e.g., requiring monitoring or imposing a compliance program). Through this kind of approach, agencies can help make it clear that a company's diligence in preventing and detecting wrongdoing truly does go to the heart of organizational culpability.

Show Through the Enforcement Process That C&E Really Does Matter

A government policy that sits on the shelf and is ignored in practice has no real value. Once the government has articulated the right policies, the next indispensable step is to apply those policies to actual cases, and to do so in a highly visible way. This means that enforcement agencies need to document and communicate, through specific cases, that preexisting C&E programs with empowered CECOs really do matter, that these programs play a specific role in enforcement decisions, and that this role is independent of how much a company subsequently cooperates during an investigation.

Focus on What's Real and Important in C&E Programs

When the government provides benefits to companies with diligent C&E programs, those companies and programs need to be demonstrably diligent. The government, in making this determination, must itself have credibility so companies know that their commitment to C&E performance has to be a serious one. To be credible, the government needs access to appropriate expertise to conduct a valid C&E program assessment. In turn, such an assessment needs to focus on C&E program elements that matter and not on merely formalistic criteria, such as codes and training lectures. For example, one element that the government should assess is whether a company has a CECO who is empowered, independent, sufficiently resourced, and connected to executive power. The role of the CECO is a prime indicator of program rigor, because without powerful leadership and expertise for the program, nothing else matters. Formal checklists can readily be developed to support the assessment of this and other C&E program elements.

Send a Single, Coherent Message

Finally, there is a need for government to speak with one clear and coherent voice on C&E issues. Among the agencies concerned with private-sector C&E programs and enforcement, there should be a strong effort to coordinate enforcement approaches. Related harmonization efforts should also be pursued on an international basis. U.S. government agencies, meanwhile, should take the further step of applying C&E best practices to their own operations.

Government exists to benefit the people. The interest of the people is not to ambush companies with larger and larger fines for misconduct but instead to prevent violations in the first place. The public and the government have much to gain when companies and other organizations actively join the fight against corporate crime and wrongdoing. To get this point across, the government must institute a strong policy, holding companies that fail to join the fight strictly accountable for their crimes. But to be fair and to encourage self-policing, it must make clear that those who join the fight are welcomed and will see the benefit of their good-faith efforts.

3. HOW MUCH PROGRESS HAVE COMPANIES MADE IN MEETING THE CULTURAL GOALS OF THE FEDERAL SENTENCING GUIDELINES FOR ORGANIZATIONS?

OVERVIEW

The second session of the symposium addressed a series of basic questions about the nature and extent of corporate progress in fulfilling the ethical culture mandates of the FSGO. The session opened with some observations on the importance of ethical culture as an adjunct to formal corporate compliance efforts. It was noted that there is no simple set of controls that can fully prevent occurrences of rule-breaking in a large organization and that "culture" represents a shared commitment to good behavior that goes beyond the technical exercise of simply parsing and obeying the law. Participants also concluded that "every employee in the corporation, from the shipping clerk to the lead director," has a role to play in contributing to this kind of culture. One participant cited an example in which an executive secretary received an anonymous package of stolen trade secrets from a corporate competitor and immediately took it to the general counsel—without reading the contents or passing the package to her own supervisor. The participant stated that this was both the right thing to do and something that helped safeguard the company from potentially significant exposure during a subsequent outside investigation. It also reflected the influence of a strong culture and shared ethical commitment within that company. A question was then posed: How can corporate leaders go about cultivating these sorts of shared values and commitments within their own organizations?

Participants in the session expressed a range of opinions about the extent to which the FSGO had been successful in prompting real improvements in corporate cultures. Some argued that considerable progress had been made by companies in meeting specific compliance program standards under the FSGO and that this progress, together with the new focus on culture, has had a positive (though difficult to quantify) impact on the field. Others expressed more mixed views. One observed that high-profile corporate efforts to suppress and punish internal whistleblowers continue to abound despite the FSGO, adding that such actions run counter to efforts to develop stronger ethical cultures. Another participant suggested that many CEOs and boards continue to prioritize short-term performance, a move that often fails to accommodate initiatives to foster stronger cultures. In such cases, related structural problems in governance and performance incentives can undermine the impact of the FSGO. Still other participants observed that it is difficult even to analyze a specific corporation's "culture," and, consequently, the influence of the FSGO in contributing to more ethical environments is difficult to quantify. Several participants also noted that an indeterminate but significant number of firms have fallen short of implementing rigorous compliance programs based on

FSGO standards. In turn, such firms are unlikely to have experienced much of an impact on their cultures as a result of the FSGO.

The discussion generated several points of agreement among participants:

- Effective C&E programs and strong organizational cultures are deeply connected.
- In some important and practical ways, corporate ethical culture can be measured.
- Corporate boards have a central role to play in building stronger ethical cultures.
- Top executives also have a key role in building stronger ethical cultures.
- Culture is the "missing link" that drives employee behavior, including the decisions of internal whistleblowers to come forward or stay silent.

EFFECTIVE COMPLIANCE AND A STRONG ORGANIZATIONAL CULTURE ARE DEEPLY CONNECTED

Several participants made the observation that effective compliance and good organizational culture are really two sides of the same coin, or else that the aim of achieving effective compliance is unlikely to be met unless an organization also has a strong ethical culture. One participant stated that "compliance is not enough. Without a positive and transparent corporate culture, management will always focus on results without concern about the means." According to another, "The big problem is that, for most companies and even regulators, the word *compliance* is seen solely as a legal issue—which completely misses the significance of culture. Culture, or 'the way things are actually done around here,' is what really drives behavior, rather than formal codes of conduct." Participants broadly agreed that there is, indeed, something fundamental and powerful about organizational culture, and about the collective norms and values of the people working for a company, in helping to protect that company from internal misconduct and wrongdoing. Culture in this sense goes beyond the narrowly technical side of compliance, which is often more focused on parsing, following, and enforcing specific rules. David Gebler touched on this in his invited remarks, noting that executives "cannot mandate a corporate culture directly, but [they] can encourage and shape a positive culture through their behavior as managers."

In a somewhat different vein, a participant observed that the FSGO was broadly conceived with the prescriptive intent of preventing crimes by influencing organizational culture, even apart from the 2004 amendment that explicitly added "culture" to the text of the guidelines. By extension, many of the FSGO provisions that define the elements of an effective compliance program are potentially influential not only because they directly address the structure of the compliance function but because they establish shared expectations and behaviors for corporate employees. Several other participants made related observations, suggesting that an empowered CECO was a key indicator of ethical culture in a firm and that corporate commitment to protecting internal whistleblowers is a similarly important indicator of good culture. One culminating observation was that the role of the CECO, and the C&E function as a whole, ought to be viewed more broadly than as just a safeguard to enforce the legal aspects of compliance. Given that ethical culture has the potential to help protect firms against misconduct and bad behavior, strong CECOs and C&E programs ought to be directly concerned with fostering good culture as well.

CORPORATE ETHICAL CULTURE CAN BE MEASURED

Some participants noted the difficulty in pinpointing exactly what an "ethical" corporate culture really is and whether its meaning is truly consistent across different organizations (or across different parts of the world). One person observed that ethical values have a lot more to do with how an individual was raised than with the setting in which he or she works and that not everyone shares the same values. Still another suggested that it can be difficult to measure corporate ethical culture, in part because there is no simple answer or explicit consensus on what it means for an organization to be "ethical." Likewise, it was suggested that *culture* is, itself, an ambiguous term—and one not easily defined or subject to formal measurement. Finally, one participant commented that executives are often at a loss as to how to promote ethical culture within their organizations, in part because they do not really understand what that involves.

Several participants, in turn, made contrasting arguments. One suggested that the practical way to address culture involves sidestepping questions of moral philosophy and focusing instead on employee behavior. What makes it possible for some employees to feel safe in coming forward within their companies to report problems? And what are the factors that tend to prevent employees from doing so? In a related vein and building on his invited remarks, David Gebler suggested that this focus on desired behaviors and roadblocks could make "culture" far more tangible and easier to measure and manage. Another participant observed that the challenges involved in measuring culture are frequently overblown, adding that two of the key measurement technologies are "lunch and beer." In other words, it is not necessarily difficult to get employees to talk informally about the culture of their own organizations, and tapping that kind of water-cooler knowledge can be an early warning system and a very valuable source of information for managers.

Other participants in the symposium suggested that formal methods and metrics for gauging corporate culture are actually fairly well developed and typically draw on a combination of survey and focus group approaches. One person observed that the most basic problem facing management is not the inability to measure relevant aspects of corporate ethical culture but, rather, a lack of commitment to actually follow through in doing so, particularly in the course of conducting periodic risk assessments and evaluating C&E program efficacy. The participant concluded that it is a signal of both poor risk management and poor culture when cultural self-assessment practices are omitted from a C&E program: "If you're not managing your culture, then your culture is surely managing you."

CORPORATE BOARDS HAVE A CENTRAL ROLE TO PLAY IN BUILDING STRONGER ETHICAL CULTURES

One major topic of conversation during the symposium involved the appropriate role of the board of directors in contributing to corporate ethical culture. Patrick Gnazzo and Keith Darcy set the stage for this conversation through their opening remarks: "Boards should be viewed as the primary sentinel for ethical culture in their organizations, [in part] because boards have longer tenure and more continuity of perspective than do CEOs. Boards have both the position and responsibility to ensure that ethical corporate culture does not erode when CEOs change." Several participants picked up on this theme and asserted that boards ought to be directly involved in monitoring and promoting good culture and that this follows from the basic fiduciary duty of directors to oversee management, as well as C&E practices, within the firm. In a related vein, other participants observed that the board of directors is ultimately the group that sets the "tone at the top" of the organization; thus, it serves to establish a corporation's culture, both by carrying out specific oversight responsibilities and by modeling high standards of personal conduct in the boardroom itself. One person offered the caution, however, that having directors with strong personal integrity is not enough to ensure a strong ethical culture within a firm, adding that board responsibilities for monitoring culture go beyond simply setting a positive "tone at the top." Finally, it was noted that boards have faced increasing legal obligations and outside expectations to monitor both C&E practice and risk management. A complementary focus on corporate culture and ethics follows as a natural extension of these elements of board responsibility. As one participant concluded, "Going forward, compliance and culture will need to be taken seriously as an assignment by corporate boards."

Given that C&E and ethical culture are an important focus for board monitoring and fiduciary duty, another question that arose during the discussion involved how boards can better address these concerns going forward. Some participants suggested that the best way would be to add to the board a director with a formal background in C&E, in much the same way that boards already include directors with financial, legal, and operational experience. One route for pursuing this aim could be to revise the stock exchange listing standards for public companies to require the addition of board members with C&E backgrounds. One participant went even further, suggesting that it would ideally be desirable to include multiple directors with C&E backgrounds on any given corporate board so that the focus on compliance and culture is not viewed as the primary purview of a single individual. Another symposium participant disagreed, however, and emphasized the governance problems posed by new mandates to add board members with specific types of expertise, including C&E. Alternative suggestions for strengthening board oversight included more training for boards on C&E and cultural issues, designating the outside lead director as a focal point for ensuring strong C&E oversight at the board level, and strengthening the reporting relationship between boards and CECOs to ensure that unfiltered information about C&E program performance and the corporate culture is brought to the attention of the board on a regular basis.

TOP EXECUTIVES ALSO HAVE A KEY ROLE IN BUILDING STRONGER ETHICAL CULTURES

Another significant theme of the discussion involved the role of top management figures in driving a strong ethical culture. One person observed that the corporate CEO has to be involved in helping to build and model the corporate ethical culture and in articulating the basic values of the organization. Another said, "CEOs have lots of short-term demands, but they must also build ethical conduct into job performance for everyone." Several participants commented on the basic cultural problems that CEOs often face, as well as their own vulnerability to being influenced by organizational culture, sometimes in undesirable ways. "Too many CEOs engage in self-deception," said one participant, commenting on the tendency of many top executives to ignore or subordinate concerns about ethical culture while prioritizing short-term financial performance. On a related note, another stated, "CEOs cannot be willfully blind about what it takes to succeed," referring to the potential for unintended behavioral consequences of encouraging a tunnel-vision focus on the bottom line. Still another participant observed that "good corporate cultures and sound ethical leadership are the same thing" and suggested that a strong ethical culture can only emerge with the commitment and informed involvement of the top executive and his or her leadership team. Finally, David Gebler picked up more broadly on the role of leadership in fostering ethical culture, building on his invited remarks: "There are many workplace interventions that executives and managers can undertake to improve corporate culture and address the 'slippery slope,' but doing so requires commitment, knowledge, and appropriate training."

CULTURE IS THE "MISSING LINK" THAT DRIVES EMPLOYEE BEHAVIOR, INCLUDING THE DECISIONS OF INTERNAL WHISTLEBLOWERS TO COME FORWARD OR STAY SILENT

Another theme of the discussion touched on both culture and compliance as they relate to the link between corporate ethical culture and the success or failure of internal reporting mechanisms. One symposium participant said that internal compliance reporting procedures and hotlines perform as intended only when employees feel safe using them, adding, "You can lead a horse to water, but you can't make it call the compliance helpline." By extension, when employees view a corporate commitment to protecting and listening to internal whistleblowers as hollow, they will be less likely to report internal problems, and the organizational culture will suffer accordingly. Another participant pointed out that large corporations too often adopt a self-contradictory posture when it comes to protecting and defending internal whistleblower reporting channels—a move that was described as self-sabotage and corrosive to a positive ethical culture. Still another observed that two of the basic values that animate a strong ethical culture are integrity and transparency. A lack of a serious commitment to honoring and protecting internal reporting processes signals to employees that integrity and transparency are not strongly regarded by the organization. This can, in turn, have a range of negative consequences for employee behavior, with unwillingness to come forward and report on compliance problems and instances of misconduct being only one example.

4. WHAT ARE THE BARRIERS TO ACHIEVING STRONGER ETHICAL CULTURES AND MORE EFFECTIVE C&E PROGRAMS IN FIRMS, AND WHAT SHOULD BOARDS, MANAGEMENT, AND POLICYMAKERS DO NEXT?

OVERVIEW

In the final session of the symposium, participants focused more deeply on the aim of improving ethical culture and C&E efforts within firms and on identifying tangible next steps that could help in pursuing those ends. The session opened with some reflections on the high-profile breakdown of ethical culture at WorldCom more than a decade ago, which ultimately led to the collapse of that company. Participants noted that the deficiencies at WorldCom did not stem from an isolated accounting problem or single rogue executive but, rather, from a more entrenched set of shortcomings that involved multiple gatekeepers and executives who did not carry out their responsibilities. Other contributing factors included a lack of transparency and information-sharing between senior management and the board, the corrosive influence of excessive greed among some top executives, and a collective failure to carry out the company's fiduciary duty to shareholders. The problems at WorldCom were described as "cultural" (in the sense that they were deep and widespread), reflecting a lack of "tone at the top," and perverting controls and corporate governance mechanisms that, on paper, should have helped to prevent the breakdown. The discussion touched on the policy response to the company's collapse as well: The subsequent Sarbanes-Oxley (SOX) legislation included multiple provisions designed to address specific problems that were revealed by the scandals at WorldCom. Without commenting directly on the success of SOX, however, it was suggested that progress in addressing the deeper cultural challenges illustrated by WorldCom's failure would likely require a new and different type of commitment from boards and management.

Much of the session's discussion addressed how to facilitate this kind of cultural change within corporations and how to overcome existing corporate barriers. Some participants focused on how law and policy might be used to try to promote these ends and whether it would be appropriate to expand or refine the FSGO. Jeff Kaplan's invited remarks helped frame this conversation, suggesting that "C&E law currently stands at a crossroads," and that "the promise of the FSGO in strengthening C&E and culture can only be fulfilled through [continued and more strategic] efforts on the part of policymakers, boards, and management."

Other strands of the discussion focused more on specific actions that boards and senior management could take to foster stronger cultures within their organizations. It was noted that a significant part of the challenge lies simply in convincing top executives and boards to *want* to advocate for stronger ethical cultures. Participants agreed that the ties between a deficient ethical culture and lapses in compliance, and between lapses in compliance and reputational risk, are an important part of the calculus in making the case for stronger C&E programs to executives and boards. Participants also observed that a central challenge involves overcoming the perception that ethical culture and behavior are either easy or prohibitively difficult to cultivate within an organization. In the end, the discussion emphasized of the need to identify some concrete steps to overcome both forms of inertia. One participant noted that corporate boards and executives too often believe that "tone at the top" is about talk rather than action and lack insight into specific interventions that might support better culture: "If you are not managing culture, then culture is managing you."

The session's discussion highlighted the following areas of agreement among participants:

- An independent, empowered CECO is a key ingredient in achieving a stronger ethical culture.
- Performance incentives offer a critical tool for driving ethical culture as a priority within organizations.
- Companies need to commit to periodic self-assessments of ethical culture as a part of their C&E programs.
- Policymakers should reward companies for implementing superior C&E programs and cultures while punishing deficiencies.
- Boards and executives need to grapple with the value proposition for a strong ethical culture.
- Firms need to overcome a legalistic, check-the-box view of compliance.

AN INDEPENDENT, EMPOWERED CECO IS A KEY INGREDIENT IN ACHIEVING A STRONGER ETHICAL CULTURE

One of the top identified steps for strengthening both the C&E function and corporate ethical culture involved appointing an empowered CECO, someone with sufficient independence, mandate, and resources to carry out C&E program responsibilities effectively. One symposium participant said, "The independence and positioning of the chief compliance officer is the number one leading indicator of C&E program effectiveness, and of how seriously management views the issues of culture and compliance." Another participant observed that the CECO is not only the person who drives the day-to-day activities of the C&E program, but he or she is the natural focal point for efforts to assess and promote ethical culture within the firm. Others commented on the fact that the past decade of amendments to the FSGO have simultaneously emphasized (1) the importance of ethical culture as a part of an effective compliance program and (2) the need to ensure that the person designated to lead the day-to-day operations of the compliance program has access to the board of directors and sufficient independence fully to execute the CECO role. These two points are not unrelated provisions in the FSGO, and structuring the CECO role appropriately does, in fact, directly support subsequent efforts to pursue a strong ethical culture within a corporation.

In a related vein, several symposium participants noted that "the compliance officer must have a seat at the table" and that "the CECO must be empowered through job security." These sorts of comments harkened back to the notion that the CECO role is partly defined by what a C&E program is supposed to accomplish. If the aim of the program includes influencing ethical culture throughout an organization by engaging and educating top management figures, collecting self-assessment data on a regular basis and sharing it with the board, and asking probing ethical questions about corporate strategy and operations, then the CECO *must* be positioned to do all of those things effectively. If the CECO is going to serve as the champion for protecting the internal reporting process, and for making it safe for employees to come forward when something goes wrong within the company, then the CECO must be protected from retaliation for asking difficult questions or "being the bearer of bad news" when allegations of misconduct arise. If the CECO is to "play the role of the court jester" by raising basic questions about the way business is done and articulating C&E issues that others are afraid to raise, then the CECO needs to have access to the C-suite and the confidence that he or she will be listened to. Symposium participants thought that these kinds of observations about the relationship between CECOs and ethical culture suggested a range of specific steps for strengthening both. Among the examples discussed were protecting CECO independence by making a CECO's termination subject to board vote; ensuring that CECOs have senior executive status themselves, giving them direct access to other senior executives in the C-suite; and making the CECO independent of other silos of executive authority, such as those of the general counsel's office or the human resources department.

PERFORMANCE INCENTIVES OFFER A CRITICAL TOOL IN FOSTERING ETHICAL CORPORATE CULTURES

Another point of discussion involved financial incentives and executive compensation as a barrier to, and potential leverage point for, more effective ethical cultures within corporations. Several participants commented that bottom-line performance pressure for executives, together with related compensation incentives, pose a fundamental challenge to many organizations. Such pressure sometimes drives management to sacrifice competing values and considerations in favor of meeting short-run targets for quarterly profits. One of the downsides to this kind of incentive structure and corporate culture is that C&E considerations are unlikely to be viewed as a high internal priority. In this regard, one symposium participant said, "Ethics is a business decision; companies need to undertake self-study to determine what kinds of [employee and executive] behaviors it is that they [want to] reward and [actually do] reward." Another emphasized the importance of clawback provisions in executive compensation as a way to punish instances of bad behavior and misconduct. Still another participant related the story of a specific organization that modified its compensation structure to make part of the annual bonus for each manager contingent on meeting a set of C&E targets within the scope of his or her responsibility. Far greater attention and concern for C&E performance was generated among managers after a set of corresponding financial incentives was built into their compensation packages. One participant observed that implicit incentives are built into many other facets of a

C&E program's structure, such as an internal reporting mechanism, which can then have potent effects (both good and bad) in influencing employee and executive behaviors.

More generally, it was acknowledged that one of the most basic devices for shaping workplace behavior involves rewarding managers and employees for what you want them to do and punishing them for what you do not want them to do—a general principle that can be aligned with improving C&E performance. And as one participant observed, instituting related incentives is another way for a corporation to demonstrate its commitment and integrity in standing behind its values and promoting corporate ethical culture.

COMPANIES NEED TO COMMIT TO PERIODIC SELF-ASSESSMENTS OF ETHICAL CULTURE AS A PART OF THEIR C&E PROGRAMS

A basic observation about corporate ethical culture was that the commitment to actually assess it is an important precursor to managing it effectively, and culture can be measured in various ways. Moreover, the act of measurement itself is arguably a signal of a strong ethical culture. As one symposium participant said, many corporations do not engage in enough self-study and thus often neglect to ask the right behavioral questions about employees and management when it comes to assessing their own cultures: "Why do the same companies get into trouble repeatedly? Why are executives and boards blind to vulnerabilities in their own cultures that can shelter or even encourage misconduct?" The simple exercise of having boards and top executives engage in reflective self-assessment, together with formal, firm-wide cultural assessments, should be a regular part of C&E programs and are basic steps in building stronger corporate ethical cultures. In a related vein, one symposium participant pointed out the importance of getting firms to "reverse engineer their compliance program failures," to understand and take action to remedy them. By extension, this same kind of reverse engineering could also provide key insights about deficits in organizational culture, as well as the enduring behavioral problems and maladaptive pressures that can sometimes lead employees to misconduct and criminality. Another symposium participant stated that, in instances of high-profile corporate scandal, it is not uncommon for boards to have "missed" problems of cultural deterioration while nominally focusing on narrower issues and problems of technical governance: "It's not rocket science. If a board makes compliance and ethics a priority and wants to get reporting on that—just like they get reporting on financial records—and asks for standard assessment practices around it, then that's a good way to ingrain [a strong focus on C&E and ethical culture] into the organization. And the board needs to evaluate management partly on that basis."

POLICYMAKERS SHOULD REWARD COMPANIES FOR IMPLEMENTING SUPERIOR C&E PROGRAMS AND CULTURES WHILE PUNISHING DEFICIENCIES

Another strand of discussion involved the question of what policymakers can and should be doing, given the aim of promoting stronger ethical cultures in corporations going forward.

Some of the comments on this point focused on various ways to strengthen board expertise and oversight of C&E, or to improve the structure of the C&E function and empowerment of the CECO, implicitly by tying specific reform measures or new mandates to criminal sentencing standards, such as the FSGO, corresponding prosecutorial guidance documents, or legislative enactments (e.g., SOX). Furthermore, as several symposium participants noted, it can be tremendously influential when law enforcement authorities make the decision not to prosecute or punish a corporation based on its strong C&E program and then publicize that decision in a way that rewards good C&E practice and a good culture. Many of the other ideas that were independently raised in the symposium session were also identified as potential targets for new policy and law enforcement interventions, including the design of C&E-friendly executive compensation packages and financial incentives, the provision of relevant training opportunities related to C&E and ethical culture for board members and top executives, and the practice of undertaking regular cultural and C&E program assessments. Discussion on these matters ultimately returned to a point that Joseph Murphy initially made in his invited remarks: "A government policy that sits on the shelf but is ignored in practice has no real value. Once government has articulated the right policies, the indispensible next step will be to apply those policies in a highly visible way in the real world."

BOARDS AND EXECUTIVES NEED TO GRAPPLE WITH THE VALUE PROPOSITION FOR A STRONG ETHICAL CULTURE

A notable theme of the discussion involved the argument for why considerations about ethical culture are a worthy focal point for boards and top executives. Several participants noted that the primary aim of any private-sector corporation is to make a profit and to generate a return for shareholders. One person posed the question of whether ethical culture problems really have much impact on reputational risk and the corporate bottom line in a firm that is otherwise operating a very successful and legitimate business—with Apple and the recent allegations of poor labor conditions in overseas factories being cited as the counterexample. According to another, "You can't legislate trust," and "the focus in business is always going to be on maximizing profits and [for the board] protecting shareholder value." By extension, profit motive and fiduciary considerations are unlikely to ever be subordinated to the pursuit of an ethical corporate culture, nor should they be, given the fundamental purpose that corporations serve. This being said, several other symposium participants noted that there have been plenty of examples of corporations in which ethical culture problems and deficient C&E programs led to significant operational and reputational risks—and eventually to catastrophic scandals and losses in shareholder value—with WorldCom again being a chief illustration. One participant suggested that the recent focus in many companies on reputational risk reflects an emerging insight that problems in culture and C&E have the potential to dramatically affect the value of a corporation in negative ways and that assessing and understanding those risks is an important part of safeguarding shareholder interest.

Participants also expressed two conflicting views about how to reconcile profit motive and concerns about ethical culture. One viewpoint was that the essential challenge in getting executives and boards to "buy into" ethical culture is to demonstrate the value proposition and to show that dollars spent on improving culture yield a direct return on investment. A competing perspective was that ethical culture, and concerns about ethical values more broadly, represent an irreducible commitment within the corporation to something that goes beyond considerations of shareholder value. Without reconciling those two points of view, another participant brought the conversation back to the notion that ethical culture is most essentially about understanding the behavioral dynamics of the corporate workplace, as well as the psychological factors that either give rise to bad behavior and misconduct or (sometimes) prevent employees from exhibiting more desirable behaviors. Again, this focus on workplace culture sidesteps some of the abstract considerations of moral philosophy in favor of trying to better engage employees and to build on their perceptions of commitment, integrity, and transparency in the workplace. It was suggested that this kind of cultural focus and change is both desirable as an end in itself and as a potentially important contribution to the enhancement of shareholder value.

FIRMS NEED TO OVERCOME A LEGALISTIC, CHECK-THE-BOX VIEW OF COMPLIANCE

Finally, a recurring theme in the session involved the notion that effective C&E efforts and programs need to go beyond the simple legalistic exercise of parsing and following rules. One participant suggested that the word *compliance,* itself, had become an impediment to strong C&E programs and ethical culture:

> The Federal Sentencing Guidelines did good things for us by bringing compliance issues to the forefront, but *compliance* is not a [purely] legal term. If we limit compliance solely to its legal aspect, then we're only going to focus on things like the FCPA and not on other core value issues and challenges within the corporation. What's the purpose of even having a corporate mission statement if we're just going to reduce that mission to maximizing shareholder value? An effective C&E program and a strong corporate ethical culture are about achieving whatever the company says its values are.

On a related point, another participant alluded to the problem of hollow or "check-the-box" C&E programs that have proliferated in some organizations and in which the entire compliance activity becomes dominated by the superficial exercise of meeting the paper requirements of SOX and the FSGO—an approach that does not have much substantive impact on actual corporate behavior. One of the central challenges in making C&E programs more effective involves overcoming a check-the-box mindset and the view that C&E is primarily about using a mechanical process to meet outside legal mandates, as opposed to cultivating deeper behavior change and ongoing self-assessment throughout the firm. Taken in this light, many of the revisions to the FSGO and efforts to empower CECOs have sought to counter a narrowly technical view of C&E and to give real weight and impact to C&E programs. One symposium participant observed that the specific FSGO mandate on corporate ethical culture speaks to this same issue and to the need to refocus C&E programs on the pursuit of deep behavioral changes in the organizations that house them. Said another participant, "Until tone at the top and corporate [ethical] culture are taken as serious responsibilities by boards of directors and management, we're not going to see real progress in preventing new episodes of high-profile scandal and abuse."

APPENDIX A: SYMPOSIUM AGENDA

Center for Corporate Ethics and Governance

A RAND INSTITUTE FOR CIVIL JUSTICE CENTER

Corporate Culture and Ethical Leadership Under the Federal Sentencing Guidelines:
What Should Boards, Management and Policymakers Do Now?

RAND Corporation, Pentagon City
1200 South Hayes Street, Arlington, VA 22202; Tel: (703) 413-1100
May 16, 2012

Symposium Chair: Dr. Michael D. Greenberg
Symposium Co-Chair: Donna C. Boehme

Agenda

1:00 p.m.   **Welcome and Introductory Remarks**

Michael D. Greenberg, Director, RAND Center for Corporate Ethics & Governance
Donna C. Boehme, Principal, Compliance Strategists, LLC

1:10 p.m.   **Invited Remarks from White Paper Authors**

Introductions by Donna C. Boehme, Principal of Compliance Strategists LLC

- Semi-Tough: A Short History of Compliance and Ethics Program Law

    Jeff Kaplan, Partner, Kaplan & Walker

- The Start of the Slippery Slope: Why Leaders Must Manage Culture to Create a Sustainable Ethics and Compliance Program

    David Gebler, President, Skout Group

- Preventing Corporate Crime: What Boards and Management Should Do Next to Support Ethical Culture and Stronger C&E Programs

    Patrick J. Gnazzo, Former SVP and General Manager, U.S. Public Sector, CA, Inc., and Principal, Better Business Practices LLC

    Keith Darcy, Executive Director, Ethics and Compliance Officer Association

- Over 20 Years Since the Federal Sentencing Guidelines: What Government Can Do Next to Support Effective Compliance and Ethics Programs

    Joseph Murphy, Director of Public Policy, Soc. for Corporate Compliance and Ethics

2:00 p.m.   **Roundtable Session 1:** How Much Progress Have Companies Made in Meeting the Culture Goals Set Out by the Federal Sentencing Guidelines for Organizations?

Introduction by Larry Thompson, former U.S. Deputy Attorney General

3:15 p.m.   **Break**

Center for Corporate Ethics and Governance

A RAND INSTITUTE FOR CIVIL JUSTICE CENTER

3:25 p.m.   **Roundtable Session 2:** What Are the Barriers to Achieving Stronger Ethical Culture and Programs in Firms, and What Should Boards, Management and Policymakers Do Next?

Introduction by Dick Thornburgh, former U.S. Attorney General and Governor of Pennsylvania

4:40 p.m.   **Closing Remarks**

Michael D. Greenberg, RAND Corporation

5:00 p.m.   **Reception** *(concluding at 6:00 p.m.)*

APPENDIX B: SYMPOSIUM PARTICIPANTS

CORPORATE CULTURE AND ETHICAL LEADERSHIP UNDER THE FEDERAL SENTENCING GUIDELINES: WHAT SHOULD BOARDS, MANAGEMENT AND POLICYMAKERS DO NOW?
Roundtable Conference
RAND Center for Corporate Ethics & Governance
MAY 16, 2012

SYMPOSIUM PARTICIPANT LIST

Michael Greenberg
(Symposium Chair)
Director, RAND Center for
Corporate Ethics and
Governance

Donna C. Boehme
(Symposium Co-Chair)
Principal, Compliance
Strategists LLC

Urmi Ashar
Immediate Past President,
National Association of
Corporate Directors, Three
Rivers Chapter; Trustee,
Excela Health

Stephen Cohen
Associate Director,
Enforcement Division, U.S.
Securities & Exchange
Commission

Keith T. Darcy
Executive Director, Ethics &
Compliance Officer
Association

Paula Desio
Former Deputy General
Counsel, U.S. Sentencing
Commission

Carlo di Florio
Director, U.S. Securities and
Exchange Commission, Office
of Compliance Inspections
and Examinations

Charles Elson
Edgar S. Woolard, Jr. Chair
in Corporate Governance and
the Director of the John L.
Weinberg Center for
Corporate Governance at the
University of Delaware

David Gebler
President, Skout Group, LLC

Peter R. Gleason
Managing Director and Chief
Financial Officer, National
Association of Corporate
Directors

Patrick J. Gnazzo
Former SVP and General
Manager, U.S. Public Sector,
CA, Inc.; Principal, Better
Business Practices LLC

Michael R. Gordon
Partner, K&L Gates LLP

Ellen M. Hunt
Director, Ethics &
Compliance, Office of
General Counsel, AARP

Jeff Kaplan
Partner, Kaplan & Walker

Stephen Kohn
Executive Director, National
Whistleblower Center

Joseph Murphy
Director of Public Policy,
Society for Corporate
Compliance and Ethics

Lester A. Myers
Professorial Lecturer,
Georgetown University

Larry Thompson
Former U.S. Deputy Attorney
General; Former Senior Vice
President and General
Counsel, PepsiCo

Richard Thornburgh
Of Counsel, K&L Gates LLP;
Former U.S. Attorney
General; Former Governor of
Pennsylvania

Harold J. Tinkler
Former Chief Ethics and
Compliance Officer, Deloitte
LLP and the Deloitte U.S. Firms

Kathryn Turner
Chief Executive Officer,
Standard Technology;
Director, Conoco-Philips,
Schering Plough, and
Carpenter Technology

John Steer
Former Vice Chair, U.S.
Sentencing Commission;
Former General Counsel, U.S.
Sentencing Commission

Alan Yuspeh
Senior Vice President and
Chief Ethics and Compliance
Officer, Hospital Corporation
of America (HCA Holdings,
Inc.)

APPENDIX C: INVITED PAPERS FROM PANEL PARTICIPANTS

SEMI-TOUGH: A SHORT HISTORY OF COMPLIANCE AND ETHICS PROGRAM LAW

Jeffrey M. Kaplan, Partner
Kaplan & Walker LLP

Groucho: Just how tough are you?
Chico: You pay little bit, we're little bit tough. You pay very much,
very much tough. You pay too much, we're too much tough.
—*Monkey Business*

This paper provides a short history of the compliance and ethics (C&E) program–related law and offers some thoughts about its (somewhat uncertain) future.

Background on the Federal Sentencing Guidelines for Organizations

There is no one place where the law relating to C&E programs—referred to in this paper as *C&E program law*—begins. Early antecedents include, but are not limited to, the internal controls requirements of the Foreign Corrupt Practices Act of 1977 (FCPA);[1] informal policy of the U.S. Department of Justice's Fraud Division dating back to 1988 providing that prosecutors should consider defense contractors' C&E programs in determining whether to bring charges against such organizations in criminal investigations;[2] provisions of an insider trading law passed in 1988 that created enforcement-related incentives for organizations to take preventive measures in this area;[3] and the "Star" program of the Occupational Safety and Health Administration, which provided regulatory relief to businesses that committed to taking certain strong compliance measures.[4] However, without question, the most important development in this area was the advent of the Federal Sentencing Guidelines for Organizations (FSGO) in 1991.

The FSGO were developed in response to the Sentencing Reform Act of 1984,[5] the main purpose of which was to create sentencing guidelines for individuals convicted of federal crimes. Such guidelines were promulgated in 1987 by the U.S. Sentencing Commission (USSC),

---

1 Foreign Corrupt Practices Act, Pub. L. No. 95-213, 91 Stat. 1494 (1977), as amended by the Foreign Corrupt Practices Act Amendments of 1988, Pub. L. No. 100-418, 102 Stat. 1415 (1988).

2 Memorandum by William Hendricks, Fraud Divisions Chief, to U.S. Attorneys, discussed in Kaplan and Murphy, *Compliance Programs and the Corporate Sentencing Guidelines* (rev. ed., West, 2011)

3 Insider Trading and Securities Fraud Enforcement Act of 1988, Pub. L. 100-704, 102 Stat. 4677 (1988).

4 As described in Sigler and Murphy, *Interactive Corporate Compliance: An Alternative to Regulatory Compulsion* (Greenwood 1988).

5 Sentencing Reform Act of 1984, Pub. L. No. 98-473, 98 Stat. 1987 (codified as amended in scattered sections of 18 U.S.C. and 28 U.S.C.).

which then took up the task of creating guidelines for organizations. Initially, the commission considered an "optimal penalties" approach (based on what could be considered "Chicago School" economics), which had no direct C&E program guidance or incentives.[6] But in response to lobbying by business groups, the USSC ultimately turned to a model that incented companies to develop C&E programs (called, at the time, "effective program[s] to prevent and detect criminal conduct"), principally by providing for the possibility of very large fines but also by articulating the prospect that an organization with an effective C&E program at the time of its offense could receive a substantially more lenient punishment than would otherwise be the case.

The guidelines were indeed path-breaking, not only because they provided the first broad-based incentive for organizations to implement formal C&E programs,[7] but also because they set forth governmental expectations (albeit in a broad way) of what such programs should entail—the now well-known "seven steps." These included written standards, program oversight, training, means to receive reports of suspected wrongdoing, discipline for violations, and auditing. All of these had long been, of course, a matter of sound risk management, but with the guidelines, they assumed something akin to the force of law.

The 1990s[8]

Prior to the advent of the FSGO, there were a relatively small number of companies— mostly in the United States—that had C&E programs. The guidelines prompted many such organizations to review and, as needed, revise their programs to meet the FSGO's expectations, which, in effect, became a new standard of accountability in the C&E realm. The guidelines also prompted a fair number of other companies to develop C&E programs. Reflective of these developments, the first trade association for C&E officers—the Ethics Officer Association (EOA)—was formed in 1992.[9]

Presumably owing to the fact that the FSGO penalty provisions were not applied retroactively, there were no very large fines imposed under the guidelines for several years after they went into effect. However, by the end of the decade, there had been a few, including a $100 million fine imposed on Archer Daniels Midland in 1995 (for antitrust violations), a $340 million fine on Daiwa Bank in 1996 (for banking-related offenses), and a $500 million one on Hoffman-La Roche (another antitrust case). These and other prosecutions helped make the case that developing an effective C&E program was good for business.

There were several other major law-related developments in the 1990s that contributed to the growth of C&E programs:

---

6 The history of the drafting of the guidelines can be found in Chapter 2 of Kaplan and Murphy.
7 However, the guidelines excluded antitrust offenses from such mitigation.
8 For a more detailed recounting of C&E program history during this decade see, Kaplan, "Sentencing Guidelines: The First Ten Years," *Ethikos* (November–December 2001), available at http://www.ethikospublication.com/html/guidelines10years.html.
9 Now the Ethics and Compliance Officer Association.

- The "Holder Memo," issued in 1999, which provided (among other things) that preexisting C&E programs should be considered, at least in some instances, by federal prosecutors in determining whether to bring charges against businesses. (The Holder Memo was revised in 2003 by then–Deputy Attorney General Larry Thompson, again in December 2006 by then–Deputy Attorney General Paul J. McNulty, and again in 2008, when it was incorporated into the U.S. Attorneys' Manual.)[10]
- Several decisions of the U.S. Supreme Court holding that, in certain circumstances, an organization could escape liability and/or punitive damages in hostile-environment sexual harassment cases if, among other things, it had an effective sexual harassment compliance program in place at the time of the wrongdoing.[11]
- A ruling by the Delaware Chancery Court that, broadly speaking, imposed C&E program–related fiduciary duties on corporate directors.[12]
- Several subject-matter-specific developments promoting C&E programs.[13]

During this period, C&E programs were becoming more commonplace, at least in the United States. Indeed, the EOA, which had only 12 members in 1992 when it was founded, had 632 members by 2000.[14] The country outside the United States with the strongest C&E legal regime was Australia, where a national standard for C&E programs was implemented in 1998 and applied in certain law-related contexts.[15] Also, the Canadian Competition Bureau established compliance program guidelines in 1997.[16]

2001–2004

This was the period that, by far, saw the most important legal developments in this field and that could be considered the "golden age" of C&E law. Among these developments were:

- Several landmark incidents of wrongdoing in businesses (often related to financial reporting) involving such prominent companies as Enron and WorldCom. These instances helped demonstrate the need for more preventive efforts. They also drew

---

10 *United States Attorneys' Manual*, "Principles of Federal Prosecution of Business Organizations," § 9-28.800 (2008).

11 *Faragher v. City of Boca Raton*, 524 U.S. 775 (1998); *Burlington Industries v. Ellerth*, 524 U.S. 742 (1998).

12 *In Re Caremark Int'l Inc. Derivative Litigation*, 698 A.2d 959 (Del. Ch. 1996).

13 See, e.g., Environmental Protection Agency, *Incentives for Self-Policing: Discovery, Disclosure, Correction and Prevention of Violations* (April 11, 2000), available at http://epa.gov/oecaerth/resources/policies/incentives/auditing/auditpolicy51100.pdf.

14 Kaplan, "Sentencing Guidelines: The First Ten Years."

15 See Dee, *Australian Standards on Compliance Programs* (2006).

16 These were amended in 2008. See Canadian Competition Bureau, "Corporate Compliance Programs," available at http://www.competitionbureau.gc.ca/eic/site/cb-bc.nsf/eng/02732.html.

unprecedented attention to the role of organizational culture in fostering crimes in business.[17]

- Adoption of a policy by the Securities and Exchange Commission (SEC) in 2001 that provides (among other things) for giving credit in enforcement decisions to issuers with C&E programs.[18]

- Passage of the Sarbanes-Oxley Act in 2002, which created several C&E program–related expectations for public companies.[19]

- Adoption by the New York Stock Exchange[20] and NASDAQ[21] of corporate governance listing requirements with several C&E mandates.

- Publication of highly detailed C&E program guidance from the Office of Inspector General of the Department of Health and Human Services[22] and other risk-area-specific C&E program mandates/guidance.[23]

- Enactment of laws by several states requiring sexual harassment training in business organizations.[24]

But more important than any of these, from the perspective of shaping C&E program expectations, were the 2004 revisions to the FSGO, which made the definition of an effective C&E program far more detailed and rigorous than that found in the original seven steps. Among other things, these revisions:

- Created an expectation of C&E risk assessments, which the FSGO presents as a foundational element to an effective program.

- Articulated program-related expectations of boards of directors and senior management, and also regarding day-to-day program management.[25]

- Included in the consideration of an effective C&E program an organization's culture, based, in part, on the above-mentioned lessons from Enron and WorldCom.

---

17 See *In Re WorldCom*, First Interim Report of Dick Thornburgh, Bankruptcy Court Examiner, Nov. 4, 2002, (describing a "culture of greed which may be said to have permeated top management…").

18 SEC Report of Investigation, Exchange Act Release No. 34-44969, 2001 WL 1301408, at n.3 (October 23, 2001).

19 Pub. L. 107-204, 116 Stat. 745 (2002)

20 NYSE Rule 303A.10.

21 Nasdaq Rule 4350(n).

22 Department of Health and Human Services, Office of the Inspector General's Compliance Program Guidance for Pharmaceutical Manufacturers, 68 Fed. Reg. 23,731, 23,731 (May 5, 2003).

23 Such as those related to money laundering provided by Patriot Act; Uniting and Strengthening America by Providing Appropriate Tools Required to Intercept and Obstruct Terrorism Act, Pub. L. No. 107-56, § 352(a) (2001).

24 For example, California's AB 1825.

25 Among other changes, the 2004 revisions set forth the expectation that the board must be "knowledgeable about the content and operation" and "exercise reasonable oversight with respect to the implementation and effectiveness" of the compliance program.

- Added to the purely law/compliance focus of the definition of an effective program an ethics dimension.
- Also included consideration compliance-related incentives in the definition of an effective program.
- Enhanced expectations around other program elements, such as training and communications.
- Set forth expectations regarding self-assessing the efficacy of programs.[26]

During this period, C&E program law was still largely a U.S. phenomenon, but with some exceptions. One example of what could be called the "guidelines" approach being adopted outside the United States was the passage of a statute in Italy in 2001 that created enforcement-related incentives for C&E programs—initially in the context of corruption cases but since applied to a wide variety of other areas.[27]

2005–Present

This period is much harder to categorize in any broad way than the prior ones, as there has been both forward and backward movement with respect C&E program law.

The most promising developments from this period lie in the anti-corruption realm. That is, principally due to a rapid increase in FCPA enforcement actions during this period, many companies started to create or enhance anti-corruption compliance programs, with some spillover to C&E general program areas. Among the reasons for this strong approach to anti-corruption compliance was that:

- The internal controls provisions of the FCPA make C&E directly relevant to the consideration liability.
- The prosecutors responsible for this area of law (the Department of Justice's Fraud Division) have spoken publicly about the importance of C&E programs more than have other prosecutors in other substantive areas.[28]
- Large FCPA fines[29] have made the business case for strong compliance in this area particularly compelling.

---

26 The current version of the FSGO can be found at http://www.ussc.gov/Guidelines/2011_guidelines/Manual_HTML/8b2_1.htm.

27 Bevilacqua, "Compliance Programs Under Italian Law," *Ethikos* (November–December 2006), available at http://www.ethikospublication.com/html/italy.html.

28 See Kaplan, "Credit for Compliance: The DOJ Gets Specific," *The FCPA Blog* (November 23, 2010), available at http://www.fcpablog.com/blog/2010/11/23/credit-for-compliance-the-doj-gets-specific.html.

29 A list of the largest fines under the FCPA can be found at http://www.fcpablog.com/blog/2011/4/8/jj-joins-new-top-ten.html.

- Large fines have also led to an unprecedented number of Caremark claims, which has caused corporate directors to pay greater attention to the compliance in this area.[30]

Indeed, this period also saw the imposition of other large fines, particular in the areas of pharma fraud and abuse and—both inside in the United States and elsewhere—antitrust (competition) law.[31] In a sense, then, it took about 15 years for the penalty provisions of the FSGO to fully come into play.

Additionally, developments outside the United States concerning anti-corruption enforcement and compliance have led to an unprecedented expansion of C&E programs globally. The two principal events here are:

- In December 2009, a working group of the Organisation for Economic Co-operation and Development (OECD), representing the 30 OECD member nations (including the United States) and eight other countries, issued its *Recommendation for Further Combating Bribery of Foreign Public Officials in International Business Transactions*, which, among other things, provides that member countries should encourage companies "to develop and adopt adequate internal controls, ethics and compliance programmes or measures for the purpose of preventing and detecting foreign bribery." A few months later, the working group issued the report *Good Practice Guidance on Internal Controls, Ethics and Compliance* for anti-bribery compliance programs, which, like the revised FSGO, provides considerable detail on compliance program expectations.[32]
- In 2010, a bribery act went into law in the United Kingdom that both expanded the prospect of organizational liability for corruption and incented anti-corruption compliance programs by creating a defense relating to such programs. Subsequently, the UK Ministry of Justice issued an influential anti-corruption compliance program guidance for business organizations.[33]

Another important legal development from this period was the further revision of the FSGO in 2010. While not as sweeping as the 2004 revisions, the 2010 amendments did enhance independence-related expectations for C&E officers.[34] Such expectations were also reinforced in

---

30 Grow, "Bribery Investigations Spark Shareholder Suits," Reuters (November 1, 2010), available at http://www.reuters.com/article/2010/11/01/us-bribery-lawsuits-idUSTRE6A04CO20101101.

31 A list of some of the largest federal criminal fines generally can be found at http://www.corporatecomplianceinsights.com/risk-assessment-biggest-mega-fines.

32 Available at http://www.justice.gov/criminal/fraud/fcpa/docs/oecd-good-practice.pdf. See also Boehme and Murphy, "OECD Adds Three Words to Its Anti-Bribery Recommendations," *Ethikos*, (March 2010).

33 Available at http://www.justice.gov.uk/legislation/bribery.

34 The FSGO are available at http://www.ussc.gov/Guidelines/2011_guidelines/Manual_HTML/8b2_1.htm. See also Greenberg, *Perspectives of Chief Ethics and Compliance Officers on the Detection and Prevention of Corporate Misdeeds: What*

various settlements (deferred prosecution or non-prosecution agreements) setting forth C&E program expectations of the defendant organizations.[35]

There were numerous other, subject-matter-specific legal developments that promoted C&E programs, including (but by no means limited to) those having to do with government contracting[36] and energy utilities.[37]

In a different vein, the financial meltdown of 2008 has also been important to C&E programs in two ways. First, it demonstrated how important incentives and organizational culture are to compliance risk and mitigation. Second, it led to the Dodd-Frank Act of 2010, which, among other things, involved the SEC offering large financial awards to whistleblowers in certain cases, which further enhanced the business case for strong programs.[38]

During this period, the C&E profession continued to expand, as reflected in the growing memberships of the ECOA and of a newer C&E trade organization, the Society of Corporate Compliance and Ethics.

However, as indicated above, during this period, the C&E picture became increasingly mixed. At least based on anecdotal evidence, by the end of this period, many companies had begun to cut back on their commitment to C&E programs, although obviously they did not do so in any public way.

Some observers believe that the problem lies with government agencies that (with the above-noted exception of the Fraud Division of the Justice Department) have failed to provide any meaningful indication that effective C&E programs do in fact matter in enforcement decisions. This has been examined in detail in a 2009 report by the Conference Board[39] and a 2011 draft report by the Ethics Resource Center.[40]

In effect, while the FSGO C&E program provisions are clearly tough as written, as applied, they may more accurately be characterized as only semi-tough. And, to follow the "Marxist" economic logic at the beginning of this paper (meaning Chico, not Karl), this has caused many C&E programs to be only semi-effective.

---

the Policy Community Should Know, RAND Corporation, CF-258-RC (2009), available at http://www.rand.org/pubs/conf_proceedings/CF258.html.

35 See, e.g., the corporate integrity agreement involving Eli Lilly and Company, available at http://lilly.com/Documents/CIA.pdf.

36 FAR 52.203-13.

37 Federal Energy Regulatory Commission, Revised Policy Statement on Enforcement, Docket No. PL08-3-000, par. 57-60 (May 15, 2008).

38 Pub. L. No. 111-203, § 922(a), 124 Stat. 1376 (2010). Under section 922 of the Dodd-Frank Act, the SEC is required to pay cash bounties of 10–30 percent of a recovery to a whistleblower who provided original information concerning any violation of securities laws that results in a recovery of more than $1 million.

39 Berenbeim and Kaplan, *Ethics and Compliance Enforcement Decisions — The Information Gap,* The Conference Board (2009).

40 Published May 1, 2012, available at http://fsgo.ethics.org/FSGO.

Yet at the same time that some companies have cut back on C&E, others have developed programs of unprecedented scope and rigor. These tend to be organizations that do business in highly regulated areas, and also companies whose managements and boards truly understand the business case for strong C&E. The hallmarks of such organizations include paying real attention to promoting an ethical culture and, in some instances, appointing an independent C&E officer.

So, in 2012, we are in a world of increasing divide between C&E "haves" and "have-nots."

Conclusion: What Lies Ahead for C&E Law

I basically see two possible scenarios, with the most likely real-world outcome being some combination of both.

In the good scenario for C&E programs:

- The U.S. government finally develops a sound approach to making the most of the Guidelines and related C&E laws through, among other things, communicating about actual cases.
- The application of C&E requirements generally, and regarding culture, incentives, and independent C&E officers in particular, continues to expand in the United States (i.e., with application to other governmental bodies[41] and to other areas of law, such as antitrust).[42])
- C&E expectations continue to go global as new anti-corruption mandates expand to cover more parts of the globe.[43]
- The almost certain increase of large fines outside the United States (due to governments increasingly needing funds) leads global companies to see more clearly the economic logic of strong preventive measures.
- C&E professionals develop more compelling approaches to program design and deployment.

In the bad scenario, none of the above happens to any meaningful degree. Instead:

---

[41] For example, as New York Country District Attorney did in 2010. Memo from Chief District Attorney Daniel R. Alonso to All Assistant District Attorneys, May 27, 2010, p. 9.

[42] Murphy and Boehme, "Fear No Evil: A Compliance and Ethics Professionals' Response To Dr. Stephan," (November 2011).

43 See, for example, Organic Law 5/2010, a recent Spanish law extending the potential for criminal sanctions to organizational misconduct. See De Buerba (2012), "Prosecutor's Guidelines Spell Out Criminal Liability of Legal Entities," International Law Office, http://www.internationallawoffice.com/newsletters/detail.aspx?g=5f76fad4-4e88-4744-b7ea-2af508d3ac7f&utm_source=ilo+newsletter&utm_medium=email&utm_campaign=white+collar+crime+newsletter&utm_content=newsletter+2012-04-23 (registration required).

- The government allows C&E to be sacrificed to the cause of business necessity.[44]
- The C&E profession fails to make progress in gaining independence and developing compelling approaches to programs.
- C&E becomes absorbed into the general area of risk management, and even more programs are, in effect, "hollowed out."

As of this writing, recent news offered support for C&E pessimists and optimists alike. The former can point to the FCPA scandal involving Walmart—a company that had what seemed to be a strong C&E program—as showing the limits of internal C&E measures. But around the same time, the Justice Department and SEC took the apparently unprecedented step of publicly crediting a preexisting C&E program as a reason to decline to prosecute an organization (Morgan Stanley, in an FCPA prosecution involving one of its former employees).[45] If Justice and the SEC use this case as a model for promoting C&E programs, we could one day have a world of C&E programs that are "very much"—rather than merely being "semi"—tough.

---

44 Examples include efforts to weaken the FCPA and certain provisions of the JOBS Act.

45 See "Breakthrough: Feds Credit Morgan Stanley Compliance Program," *The FCPA Blog* (April 27, 2012), available at http://www.fcpablog.com/blog/2012/4/27/breakthrough-feds-credit-morgan-stanley-compliance-program.html.

THE START OF THE SLIPPERY SLOPE: HOW LEADERS CAN MANAGE CULTURE TO CREATE A SUSTAINABLE ETHICS AND COMPLIANCE PROGRAM

David Gebler, PresidentSkout Group, LLC[1]

Putting Culture First

Most organizational leaders now subscribe to the concept that "culture trumps compliance." But chances are they have not spent much time determining just what that means. They should. Creating an ethical culture will not only serve as the foundation for an effective ethics and compliance program, but it also serves double duty as the process to create a more profitable and sustainable culture overall.

However, an ethical culture will not emerge de facto merely by following the seven steps of the Federal Sentencing Guidelines for Organizations. Changing a culture is not accomplished by merely working through a checklist of soft-skills items. And yet, many companies act as if literal compliance with FSGO somehow sprouts an ethical culture (like a beanstalk from a magic bean). While leaders will assert that in implementing the seven steps they have done their duty to "promote an organizational culture that encourages ethical behavior and compliance with the law," this can create a false sense of security. Although leaders may want to move on to the next set priorities because compliance is "done," if the organization's expected standards of behavior are not aligned with the informal social norms that exist within the organization, then significant risks can be masked.

Culture, as we will see, is determined by what people actually do, not what they should do. Yet, many organizations do not identify and manage the underlying behaviors that actually promote an ethical culture. They identify improper behavior once it occurs but rarely identify the behavior that generates the risks in the first place.

Not only do rules not create culture, but workplace culture itself is often more potent than any rules in determining behavior. In turn, it is that workplace environment that demands management, if indeed leaders are truly intent on creating an ethical organization. To put it another way, culture is not just an additional element that companies need to concern themselves with when implementing an ethics and compliance program; it's the framework for the entire program. Get the culture wrong and nothing else matters.

And yet measuring and managing culture has been quite challenging for organizations and their leaders. It has been seen as too vague and amorphous to harness and control. What can help is to break culture down into its core components and to see how the interaction of those elements influences behavior.

---

1 David Gebler is also the author of *The 3 Power Values: How Commitment, Integrity, and Transparency Clear the Roadblocks to Performance,* Jossey-Bass, 2012.

Elements of Culture

Culture "is." Although leaders can influence culture, for better and for worse, they cannot mandate it. The organization's culture exists whether leaders acknowledge it or not. Culture is simply the way the organization operates, "the way we do things around here." It's the style of how leaders speak to employees and how things get done or not done, what leaders prioritize and value. It encompasses the social norms that dictate behavior. Cultures have both positive and negative elements. And because culture is what is really happening, as opposed to what leaders would like to be happening, culture can serve as the baseline for refining behavior that leadership wants to change.

This point warrants special emphasis, especially as it relates to the provisions in the FSGO that seek to promote an organizational culture that "encourages ethical behavior." An ethics and compliance program will only have a positive impact on the culture if the program is seen by employees as consistent with the reality they deal with day to day. If leaders respect the organization's standards and business practices and model the behaviors that are expected under those standards, then the social norms will begin to be aligned with the standards and drive a more ethical culture.

There are three core elements that define culture: the organization's mission and goals (the "what"), its principles and beliefs (the "why"), and the formal and informal standards of behavior (the "how"). Every organization has these elements, and employees can sense—even if they cannot articulate specifics—whether each of these has its own internal consistency and whether they work together or get in each other's way. Are the organization's goals consistent with employees' individual goals? Are the official standards of behavior consistent with social norms? Are individual employees' principles and beliefs supported by the organization?

Leaders committed to creating positive cultures focus on ensuring that the three elements of culture are in alignment. In positive corporate cultures, employees can feel good about themselves and their work (principles and beliefs are aligned with goals), they can raise issues and freely ask questions (principles and beliefs are aligned with standards of behavior), and they do not feel challenged by unfair or inconsistent work processes because people take personal responsibility for their actions and live up to their commitments (standards of behavior are aligned with goals).

But when some of the elements of culture are out of alignment, frustrations occur. When the principles are not in alignment with the goals, employees disengage and have a less vested interest in their work (lack of commitment). When goals move out of sync with standards, unfairness arises as managers and employees "do what they have to do" rather than what they have said they would do (lack of integrity). And when standards are out of alignment with values, employees see that the organization's actions are not consistent with its principles, and it becomes very difficult to ask uncomfortable but important questions and ensure that the truth is heard (lack of transparency).

Elements of Culture

The "What"

The "How"

The "Why"

Where do you start? The answer depends on whether the focus is on influencing the culture to drive behavior or influencing behavior to drive the culture. So what is the relationship between culture and individual behavior? The age-old question asked about culture is whether the organization's culture drives behavior or whether behavior drives culture. The answer is both. And understanding the nature of this cycle is critical to creating an ethical organization.

Culture and Behavior
Behavior-Driven Culture

In strong organizational cultures, where the goals are clear and best practices are consistent and enforced, the ability of any one person to influence the social norms of the organization is diminished.

But if the culture is weak, meaning poorly defined and not consistent throughout the organization, the actions (behaviors) of dominant personalities, whether employees or leaders, can have inordinate influence on the culture. In the vacuum of a culture where the organization's mission and goals are vague or contrary to the values embodied by the employees, personality cults can thrive, mostly by virtue of whether other leaders passively or actively condone the actions of these influencers. In some instances, these actions are positive, but usually the influence of individual behavior on the culture comes from negative behavior that challenges and then resets the social norms. The empires of middle managers flourish in the vacuum of weak organizational culture.

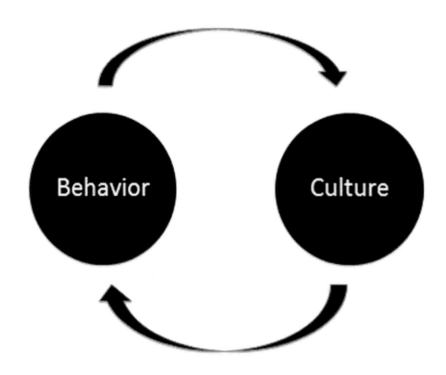

Culture-Driven Behavior

On the other hand, the prevailing social norms within the culture, whether desired or just implicit, have tremendous influence on the behavior of most of the members of the organizational community. We tend to act consistently with the norms established and condoned by peers and by leaders. If the values and the culture are not clearly stated, employees will look for cues for how to behave from their local leaders. Imagine someone's first day on the job in a company. After the formal orientation, a smart new employee will listen for cues as to how they should really act.

The impact of culture on behavior is hard for many American leaders to accept. In this society, we tend to focus on the deeds of individuals. We like to believe that we are masters of our own destiny, for better or for worse. We always see business in terms of heroes and villains. That is why we pay our CEOs so much and why we like to think that the case is closed when the guilty are punished.

But the iconic figure of the lone hero steadfast in his or her values and morals is more fiction than reality. Individual behavior is influenced as much by external environmental factors as it is by our internal sense of morality and values.

Although we would like to think that we are masters of our own decisions and actions, social norms and expectations significantly influence individual behavior. In the 1930s, Kurt Lewin, one of the pioneers of social psychology, conducted groundbreaking research on why people behave the way they do. Prior to Lewin, the prevailing theory had attributed a person's behavior to either his or her personality and character (nature) or circumstances (nurture); Lewin showed that it was both. We may therefore behave differently in different circumstances. We are neither completely good nor completely bad, and we do not always act in the most rational way. In the workplace, this means that anyone at any time can decide to engage in activities that further the company's interests or their own interests. Of course, at one end of the spectrum are sociopaths, who are not influenced by their environment, and at the other end are virtuous people, who do the right thing no matter what. But most of us are somewhere in the middle: We generally act in accordance with our personal values, but our sense of when and how to apply our values is influenced by the social norms in the workplace and the society around us.

Recent research suggests that even our own sense of right and wrong is not as fixed as we would like to think.[2] What is important for leaders to understand is that our self-concept itself can change with the circumstances—in particular, with the organizational culture. Employees who feel honest can also feel pressured, influenced, or lured by the company's culture into doing things they did not set out to do, they are not proud of, or they would not do in other circumstances. In my experience, it is as if we have a number of mental switches that turn on under certain circumstances, dangerously shifting the emphasis of our decisionmaking from the company's interest to forms of self-interest that can range from personal gain to sheer self-protection. The three most important of these switches are self-deception, rationalization, and disengagement. These basic human vulnerabilities influence the behaviors that sit at the very top of the slippery slope. As we will see, interventions that address these switches will have the greatest impact on leadership's efforts to create an ethical culture.

- Self-deception: "I think it's okay to do this." Sometimes self-deception allows us to think what we are doing is right, even though, in other circumstances (or if done by other people), we would know that it is wrong. Extreme focus on meeting a goal, for example, can cloud our view of objective facts because we have a vested interest in a particular outcome. It's human nature to discount the importance of facts that run counter to our desired outcome.
- Rationalization: "I know it's wrong, but I have a good reason for doing it." Under pressure to meet short-term goals, the right thing to do can seem wrong and the wrong thing can seem right. For audit employees at the ill-fated telecommunications company WorldCom, for example, rationalizing misdeeds was justified when

---

2 Mazar, N., Amit, O., and Ariely, D. "The Dishonesty of Honest People: A Theory of Self-Concept Maintenance," *Journal of Marketing Research*, 2008, 45, pp. 633–644.

members of the audit team allowed themselves to be convinced that what they were doing was essential for saving the company. Once this switch is flipped, flipping it back is hard.

- Disengagement: "I know there's something wrong here, but it's not my problem," or "Why should I bother trying to help? They won't listen to what I say or appreciate what I do." Companies are at risk when employees stop caring. Disengaged employees are less likely to intervene to challenge questionable business practices or to report misconduct. What keeps employees engaged? It's not just the money. Traditional rewards and punishments—raises and promotions or the denial of those things—can distort the more powerful intrinsic motivations that drive commitment: helping customers, helping one's team, or doing a job one can be proud of. In fact, traditional methods of reward can sometimes be counterproductive. And for all kinds of employees, management that is (or seems) too busy to listen or even say hello is, in fact, a serious risk factor, flipping the switch so that employees' natural impulse to contribute to the company's success is cut off; instead, it seems right not to bother.

In a healthy culture, there are means to challenge and prevent these three switches from being flipped. However, in an unhealthy culture, leaders must change their approach in order to address these switches. Old tactics focused on influencing the individual, through policies and awareness training. New approaches focus on influencing the social norms that create the cultural milieu that allows these negative forces to thrive.

A New Way of Thinking

The biggest challenge in systematically looking at culture is that the risk factors and red flags that will lead to problems manifest themselves before the bad things actually happen. In the pressure of meeting aggressive goals, most leaders and managers find themselves adhering to the strategy of "if it ain't broke, don't fix it." Therefore, leaders (who, despite rumors to the contrary, are human beings themselves and therefore are as vulnerable to denial and rationalization as anyone else) will discount the risks in the face of immediate business needs. In our normal internal decisionmaking process, we weigh the various risks and evaluate potential consequences, and then act. The immediate prospect of not meeting a goal or of gaining an immediate benefit, such as a bonus, will usually outweigh a longer-term risk or benefit. In order to change that calculation, we need to frame the risks or benefits of preventative action in ways that make it easier for individual decisionmakers to compare against short-term action or inaction. In successful ethical cultures, leaders have been trained and warned to not ignore early warning signs and those signs are treated as seriously as the misconduct that can result from them.

How can leaders and organizations adopt better means of highlighting the risks and benefits of preventative action? We need to make sure that those steps are as concrete as possible. Vague risks and benefits have a harder time competing for attention against the immediate here-and-now matters. As a first step, we need to work our way upstream to the beginning of the slippery slope, where things are murky because the risk factors are not illegal or even unethical. In fact, the issues leaders will need to address are often acceptable business practices that are of concern only because they are ripe for excess.

Get to the Start of the Slippery Slope

Policies and rules alone do not change behavior any more than posting speed limit signs ensures that every driver will obey. Policies and rules can only create expectations for behavior that will be followed or ignored. What will dictate behavior is whether the social norms of the organization are aligned with the expected behavior. These are the practices that people will follow.

To change, behavior leaders need to focus on the social norms that prevent culture alignment and what influences them. Three types of interventions have the most immediate impact on the social norms that create an ethical culture. They placate our tendencies toward self-deception, rationalization, and disengagement by bringing into alignment the three elements of culture, mission and goals, principles and beliefs, and standards of behavior.

Accountability—to Boost Integrity

Integrity links goals (what the organization strives to do) with its standards of behavior (how things are done). The organization can align its goals with its standards by insisting that its people do their jobs in a manner consistent with those goals. In parallel, the organization can ensure that both leaders and employees are "walking the talk" by insisting that people be accountable for their actions and making sure that there are consequences for failing to live up to one's commitments.

To create an ethical culture, there must be sufficient consistency and predictability in processes and in the way the organization does its work so that employees will not feel they are being treated unfairly and will begin to rationalize their actions.

Because managers have such a pervasive influence on the actions of the people who work under them, leaders must pay close attention to their own behaviors and tone that negatively impact the culture. While it is more obvious that abusive behavior from a leader will negatively impact the culture, it is often overlooked that more subtle types of behavior can impact culture as well.

For example, even when "good guys" become senior leaders, they become less approachable. Something similar happens to those who report to the leader: They don't want to be seen as "whiners." In many corporate cultures, asking questions is a sign of weakness.

Every leader needs an individual mentor or a small group who is unafraid to speak truth to power and will hold him or her accountable for his or her actions. It's a role much like that of the medieval jester in the court of the king. One of the most persistent roadblocks to establishing an ethical culture is leaders' isolation and inability to get adequate counsel on contrary opinions. While leaders may need to show confidence, there are likely to be many times when self-doubt or even fear runs through their heads. The last thing they need are yes-men or yes-women intent on pleasing the boss for their own advantage rather than telling the boss what's really going on. While most leaders will be told of ethics issues once incidents have occurred, they may not be told of cultural tensions that are leading to trouble. If it has not yet become a crisis, why should the boss be bothered?

Boards must hold leadership accountable for knowing where the organization is culturally vulnerable and what is being done to mitigate those risks.

Incentives—to Boost Commitment

Commitment links principles to goals by addressing how employees can bring their own principles to work. When those principles are aligned with the organization's goals, they feel a connection to the organization, which drives commitment. Leaders need to know whether their employees are engaged enough to be willing to report misconduct. They also need to know whether widespread disengagement has lowered the bar on the social norms that govern standards of behavior.

Incentives, both extrinsic (i.e., tangible benefits) and intrinsic (things that make us feel good about ourselves) have a tremendous influence on behavior. Inside organizations, we tend to do what we are rewarded and implicitly encouraged to do. After leaders become aware of the negative behaviors they seek to curtail, as well as the positive behaviors they seek to encourage, they must take the next step and ensure that those changes are properly incented. It is a false notion to make assumptions that people will do what is expected merely because they should. Leaders must take the burden of individual nobility off the shoulders of each individual employee and instead be sure that that desired behavior is part of the incentive structure of the organization.[3]

Speaking Up—to Boost Transparency

Transparency reveals how well the organization's standards align with its principles. Do leaders and employees at all levels act according to their own values? In other words, are people in the organization being true to themselves? If the standards are consistent with the principles, there is clarity in how the organization operates. And if employees are free to speak the truth, the organization can more easily discover where principles are in conflict and whether its own principles are really what its leaders proclaim them to be.

Creating a culture where employees feel safe to ask questions and raise issues is one of the most visible and effective contributors to an ethical culture. Even in organizations where employees would report observed misconduct, they may not feel comfortable asking questions or bringing bad news to their managers or leaders.

---

[3] See Joe Murphy's White Paper, *Using Incentives in Your Compliance and Ethics Program*, Society of Corporate Compliance and Ethics, 2011, available at http://www.corporatecompliance.org/Resources/View/smid/940/ArticleID/814.aspx.

Making It Happen

Leaders who develop the means to ensure that employees and managers at all levels are engaging in the behaviors that will increase accountability, incent the right actions, and encourage speaking up will have laid the groundwork for an organizational culture that truly encourages ethical behavior and compliance with the law. The data are clear that focusing on developing an ethical culture will decrease the risk of misconduct and reputation risk to the organization.

But will leaders do this on their own? The three categories presented above will remain high-level talk without action if leaders do not drill down and focus on specific interventions that will impact the prevailing social norms. I have found that providing an analytical approach that looks at objective data (by breaking culture down into its component elements) helps leaders become more comfortable with metrics they can measure and manage, in a manner consistent with their business style and approach. This permits leaders to delegate responsibility for addressing identified behavior risk factors at an operational level.

But leaders who are not intuitively inclined to look at culture and behavior may need an additional push. Forward-thinking boards of directors ensure and insist that leaders themselves be held accountable for moving this process forward and that they are effectively incented to engage in cultural risk management. Additionally, leaders must be required to empower a senior manager, such as the chief ethics and compliance officer, to have the permission and authority to independently speak truth to power and to advise the leadership on how to manage the "soft stuff" that sits at the very start of the slippery slope.

PREVENTING CORPORATE CRIME: WHAT BOARDS AND MANAGEMENT SHOULD DO TO SUPPORT ETHICAL CULTURE AND STRONGER COMPLIANCE PROGRAMS

Patrick Gnazzo, PrincipalBetter Business Practices, LLC
Keith Darcy, Executive DirectorEthics and Compliance Officer Association

Corporate Culture and Compliance: Where Are We Today?

In the 20+ years since the birth of the Federal Sentencing Guidelines for Organizations (FSGO),[1] companies have undertaken significant activity in developing and refining compliance and ethics (C&E) programs. That activity has been accompanied, at some organizations, by increased board oversight and accountability, the growth of a multifaceted breed of compliance and ethics professionals[2] (including a new management function headed up by a chief ethics and compliance officer, or CECO),[3] and a rich body of evolving program designs and practices, most notably involving the investigation and reporting of allegations of wrongdoing. Yet, as noted in a companion white paper,[4] all of this activity has yielded mixed results. Media headlines continue to be filled with examples of companies with seemingly well-developed C&E programs embroiled in a high-profile prosecutions or settlements arising from corporate misconduct.

Clearly there continue to be gaps, some alarmingly large, not only in how companies are "preventing and detecting" corporate crime and misconduct but also in the overall ethical culture of organizations. Moreover, as argued in another companion white paper,[5] a "check-the-box" approach to the FSGO, without a critical focus on ethical culture, is destined for failure. This paper examines what boards and management should do to take C&E programs, and the ethical culture that sustains them, to the next level of effectiveness.

The Board Must Oversee Corporate Culture

Enormous airtime has been dedicated to "tone at the top" as the single most important element of setting an ethical culture, but what does that really mean? Analysts and

---

1 For current and historical versions of the Federal Sentencing Guidelines and the FSGO, see U.S. Sentencing Commission (2012), Organizational Guidelines, available at http://www.ussc.gov/Guidelines/Organizational_Guidelines/index.cfm.

2 The rapid evolution of a robust compliance and ethics profession is reflected by the growth of two professional associations: Ethics and Compliance Officer Association and the Society of Corporate Compliance and Ethics.

3 A role that can have many different titles and job descriptions; see Murphy and Leet (2007), *Working for Integrity: Finding the Perfect Job in the Rapidly Growing Compliance and Ethics Field,* Society of Corporate Compliance and Ethics.

4 See Kaplan (2012), "Semi-Tough: A Short History of Compliance and Ethics Program Law."

5 See Gebler (2012), "The Start of the Slippery Slope: How Leaders Can Manage Culture to Create a Sustainable Ethics and Compliance Program."

commentators almost always focus on the chief executive officer (CEO) and senior management team members as the drivers of "tone" and culture but overlook the equally critical role of the board. We believe, because most board members' tenure far outlasts the tenure of most CEOs, that the board must take a more proactive role in setting the standards and foundation for ethical culture and conduct, rather than simply expecting the CEO and other senior executives to "do it their own way." What is meant by an organization's culture? Boards need to know the answer to that question, in the context of their own organizations and their purposes. Is a particular organization entrepreneurial? Does it manufacture product? If so, can the environment be impacted? And how important are quality and safety in the use of the company's products? Alternately, does the organization provide services? If so, is safety a factor as well as customer satisfaction? What is the organization's risk appetite? How important is integrity with respect to the various stakeholders? These are just a few questions that an organization and its board of directors should consider in managing and safeguarding their culture.

Why should the board be viewed as the primary sentinel for culture in the organization? Senior executives, including the CEO, change frequently during the life of an organization. If management sets the culture, then the culture may become a rapidly moving target. Board members, meanwhile, represent the shareholders (the organization's owners) and therefore have the responsibility to protect their interests. The board is both well positioned and has a fiduciary responsibility to ensure that the organization's ethical culture does not erode when CEOs (and executive priorities) change. Moreover, in today's organizations, many savvy stakeholders, including employees, customers, suppliers, and the community, will hold the organization responsible for any lack of integrity, which, in turn, can easily impact the bottom line and shareholder value. Managers may be individually held accountable for this kind of culture and reputation risk, but the board, as the organization's agent, is the ultimate safeguard for the both the cultural and financial well-being of the organization.

A culture of integrity can and should manifest in many different ways in an organization. Respect and trust for employees are important to those stakeholders. Quality, safety, and truthfulness for customers and the community are expected but not always fulfilled. Protecting the environment for the community and employees, and being a generous philanthropist, are always good for morale but carry an associated cost. Respect and honesty toward suppliers should be expected, but it is not easy and is sometimes not fully appreciated. These are just some of the cultural decisions that the board of directors should discuss and reach concurrence on with the CEO and the management team.

And how should boards ensure that their CEOs and senior management teams adhere to the culture standards they have set? Boards commonly pay management executives for performance. Contingent compensation (e.g., bonuses and stock options) based on profit, cash flow, market share, and shareholder equity are common practice. By contrast, concepts such as quality, safety, and environment are only rarely used in performance-based compensation, while integrity, respect, and trust are almost never explicitly used. However, when boards are asked why these cultural goals are not part of executive performance measurement, the answer inevitably is that they are understood to be embedded in every performance requirement. Unfortunately, integrity, respect, and trust are all too frequently assumed to be a given, just like obeying the law is an assumed behavior. The problem is that these cultural norms are not at all as common, or as easily understood, as board members have tended to assume. Boards have overlooked a simple rule: When you spell out the requirement and reward the performance, then you maximize the likelihood of generating the desired behavior. Consequently, boards ought to set the cultural tone in the organization by establishing (in collaboration with senior management) that integrity, respect, and trust will be measured in every manager's performance evaluation, compensation, and promotion opportunities.[6]

As noted below, the CEO and management must support and embed an ethical culture throughout the organization, but history and the media headlines tell us that this does not happen spontaneously. Implementation of these cultural standards must be led and managed through a specific functional organization, led by the CECO, directly reporting to the board of directors.[7] Because the CECO is responsible for implementing and overseeing the management system for preventing and detecting misconduct, the independent unfiltered relationship and reciprocal responsibility between the board of directors and the CECO is critical in order to ensure the absolute top level of ethical culture and to effectively protect the maximum shareholder value.[8]

Long gone are the days when boards could simply rely on a confidential employee hotline to raise serious organizational and culture problems to their attention. This was never enough in the first place.[9] We believe that to reach the next level of effectiveness in C&E programs, boards must become "compliance savvy" by taking proactive steps to "become knowledgeable about the content and operation" and "exercise reasonable oversight over the implementation and effectiveness of" the compliance program.[10] To accomplish this, boards need to take steps to empower their CECOs to perform the critical role we have described, and to report regularly

---

6 See Murphy (2011), *Using Incentives in Your Compliance and Ethics Program,* Society of Corporate Compliance and Ethics.

7 The CECO, and his or her critical role in leading and overseeing the company's compliance and ethics program, is examined in greater detail in Greenberg (2009), *Perspectives of Chief Ethics and Compliance Officers on the Detection and Prevention of Corporate Misdeeds: What the Policy Community Should Know,* RAND Corporation, CF-258-RC, 2009, available at http://www.rand.org/pubs/conf_proceedings/CF258.html.

8 See Darcy (2010), "Board Oversight of Compliance, Ethics, Integrity, and Reputation Risks: What Directors Need to Know," in Greenberg (2010), *Directors as Guardians of Compliance and Ethics Within the Corporate Citadel: What the Policy Community Should Know,* RAND Corporation, CF-277-CCEG, 2010, available at http://www.rand.org/pubs/conf_proceedings/CF277.html. See also Boehme (2010), "Board Engagement, Training and Reporting: Strategies for the Chief Ethics and Compliance Officer," in *The Complete Compliance and Ethics Manual,* 2nd ed., Society of Corporate Compliance and Ethics, available at http://compliancestrategists.net/sitebuildercontent/sitebuilderfiles/scce.chapter2010.pdf.

9 See Boehme (May 5, 2009), "About That Confidential Helpline. . . (An Open Letter to Boards, CEOs and Other Interested Stakeholders)," *Compliance Week,* available at http://compliancestrategists.net/sitebuildercontent/sitebuilderfiles/db-complianceweek.pdf.

10 See 2004 amendments to the FSGO.

and on an unfiltered basis (i.e., executive session), on the status of their C&E programs and on any escalated matters. And, again, boards have the additional power and responsibility to support ethical culture throughout the organization in one vitally impactful area: in determining how management is evaluated, compensated, and promoted.

Concrete steps that boards should take to safeguard and support ethical culture in their organizations include:

1. Demanding integrity as a key factor in choosing the CEO and the other members of the organization's senior management team.
2. Requiring that elements of integrity, compliance, and ethical leadership be integrated into senior management performance evaluation and compensation and promotions.
3. Approving management's proposed hiring, terms of employment, and firing of the CECO.
4. Ensuring that the CECO has senior-level positioning, empowerment, autonomy from management, and adequate budget and resources in order to perform his or her responsibilities.
5. Requesting that the CECO make in-person reports to an independent committee of the board (in executive session) at least quarterly and to be present at all of the other committee meetings.
6. Ensuring that the CECO has a "seat at the table" at key leadership meetings, including the organization's operating, strategic planning, and budget committee meetings.
7. Scheduling periodic ethics training from the CECO and requesting an overall review of the organization's C&E program at least once a year.

The CEO and Senior Management Are the Drivers of Corporate Culture

While the board is the guardian of ethical culture, the CEO and senior management team are responsible for embedding that culture throughout the organization, including through the implementation of an effective C&E program. Only when a CEO and company management view this task as an important part of their own responsibility, and not merely the CECO's task, will ethical culture be created. Time and time again, as companies become embroiled in corporate misconduct and scandals, we learn of failed internal cultures where bad behavior is either ignored or actively encouraged. Such cultures do not result from isolated or sporadic acts of misconduct, but rather from a pervasive way of doing things within the organization that is tolerated or even encouraged by management. David Myers, former controller for WorldCom, has spoken publicly about the "slippery slope" that led to his rapid adoption of the cultural norms set by leadership and those around him.[11] In contrast, when the CEO and management are consistent in their leadership of ethical culture, their behaviors and expectations flow

11 Gebler (2012), *The 3 Power Values: How Commitment, Integrity, and Transparency Clear the Roadblocks to Performance*, Jossey-Bass.

downstream to the teams under their control and ultimately cascade throughout the organization. It is only through active involvement of leadership in supporting ethical culture and the C&E program that the "slippery slope" can be stopped at the beginning, long before a WorldCom-style crisis results. Those who would engage in misconduct can be, in effect, stopped or detected by those around them where there is a strong ethical culture embedded through leadership.

But just as history has disproven the old argument that a code of conduct is not needed because "we only hire good people," the notion that corporate leaders will instinctively and consistently know how to drive ethical leadership is naïve, unreasonably optimistic, or both. It is part of the mandate of the CECO to create systems that help to drive ethical culture, and to prevent and detect misconduct. To do this, the CECO must be deeply connected to the business and top management, and to support them even as they rely upon and support him or her. In this regard, the CECO also has a critical oversight and monitoring role and is responsible for reporting directly to management, but also to the board, an unfiltered opinion on the status of the company's risks, ethical culture, and compliance activities.[12]

We have already discussed ways in which the board can encourage the CEO and senior management to undertake ethical leadership by establishing the right foundation, including appropriate incentives. The board and the CEO together can also ensure that the mandate for an empowered and independent CECO is strong and includes the necessary support for him or her to help drive and monitor ethical culture as part of running an effective C&E program. Here, again, the CECO is a linchpin and central resource for the CEO and senior executive team as well as for the board.

There are endless ways in which the CEO and management can work to embed ethical culture into the operations of the organization and to support an effective C&E program. The CECO is a good resource and coach for doing so. Some illustrative steps include:[13]

1. Act as a model, in words and actions, in support of the code of conduct (be seen consulting it).
2. Be the model in your business decisions. Turn down a trip offer from a vendor, pass on to the company a gift you received, reject a business deal if you think the ethical risks are too high, and explain your decisions.

---

12 The issues of CECO independence and reporting line have been the controversial subject of debate. See Heineman (2012), "Can the Marriage of the GC and the Compliance Officer Last?" *Corporate Counsel*, and Boehme (2012), "The Real "'Happy Marriage'" Between the GC and the Compliance Officer," *Corporate Counsel*.

13 This list is drawn from (and contains additions to) Murphy (2008), *Compliance and Ethics: How Can the CEO Make the Difference?* Society of Corporate Compliance and Ethics, available at http://ww2.corporatecompliance.org/Content/NavigationMenu/Resources/WHAT_CEO_PROMOTE_ COMPLIANCE.pdf.

3. Be the model in the compliance program. Take the training first, do the safety walk-through, call the company helpline with a question, and ask a field line manager about his or her role in the code of conduct rollout and training.

4. Actively participate in any ethical leadership training or engagement program offered by the CECO, human resources, or other functions.

5. Be vigilant in creating a transparent environment within your teams, where contrary views and raising of concerns are encouraged, not just tolerated.

6. Ensure that the CECO has independent, clout, adequate resources, and a "seat at the table" at all important leadership meetings.

7. Integrate C&E goals and actions into the annual business plan and monitor them.

8. Personally recognize outstanding C&E performance or ethical leadership.

9. Personally insist on the toughest discipline when one of the top brass breaks the rules or threatens retaliation.

10. Ask your company's suppliers to embrace your commitment to C&E, and offer your company's help for them to do this.

Conclusion

For companies to progress to the next step in their efforts to embed an ethical culture and to detect and prevent misconduct, both the board and senior management must take more proactive roles. The CECO stands ready to develop, lead, and oversee C&E activities and to advise both the board and management. But only with true engagement and consistent support from these two important constituencies[14] will the private sector reach that elusive next level of effectiveness and truly achieve the self-governance and ethical cultural standards contemplated by the FSGO.

---

14 In addition to boards and management, the role of government (the third leg of the stool) is addressed in a companion white paper, Murphy (2012), "Over 20 Years Since the Federal Sentencing Guidelines: What Government Can Do Next to Support Effective Compliance and Ethics Programs."

OVER 20 YEARS SINCE THE FEDERAL SENTENCING GUIDELINES: WHAT GOVERNMENT CAN DO NEXT TO SUPPORT EFFECTIVE COMPLIANCE AND ETHICS PROGRAMS

Joseph Murphy, Director of Public PolicySociety of Corporate Compliance and Ethics

Introduction

History teaches us that strong, effective compliance and ethics (C&E) programs do not just spontaneously emerge from the corporate world. Rather, government has consistently been a catalyst for them.[1] The Federal Sentencing Guidelines starting in 1991 are the best example of this.

Building on this history, the question we need to ask now is, How can government bring this public policy priority more fully to life? How can we bring about better, more vibrant, and more effective C&E programs and further control corporate and organizational crime and misconduct? As noted in companion white papers,[2] taking organizational compliance to the next level will demand further focus and action from boards and management, together with a more strategic, proactive approach to organizational culture. But, again, government will need to play a fundamental catalyst role by incentivizing and encouraging desired behavior.

To this end, I set out below five key steps for government to consider. These include: (1) starting with a strong, consistent policy favoring C&E programs; (2) tying this policy to enforcement decisions in a meaningful way; (3) making it clear through the enforcement and regulatory process that the policy really matters; (4) focusing on what is real in C&E programs to promote steps that actually work; and (5) sending a single, coherent message through government policy.

Start with a Strong, Consistent Policy

The policy of the Federal Sentencing Guidelines in recognizing and promoting effective corporate self-policing is strong but limited because, technically, that policy applies only at criminal sentencing. Elsewhere in government, one has to pick apart a broad range of materials and cases simply to discern what the official policy toward corporate C&E programs really is. Weak and inconsistent policies can undercut recognition of the importance of C&E programs

---

1 See the discussion in Greenberg (2009), *Perspectives of Chief Ethics and Compliance Officers on the Detection and Prevention of Corporate Misdeeds: What the Policy Community Should Know*, RAND Corporation, CF-258-RC, http://www.rand.org/pubs/conf_proceedings/CF258.html.

2 Gebler (2012), "The Start of the Slippery Slope: How Leaders Can Manage Culture to Create a Sustainable Compliance and Ethics Program"; Gnazzo and Darcy (2012), "Preventing Corporate Crime: What Boards and Management Should Do to Support Ethical Culture and Stronger Compliance Programs."

and their role in performing an essential public service. Consequently, what is most needed from government is a strong, consistent policy in support of robust C&E practice.

This message could start in the executive branch, and not just at the administrative agency level. Cabinet-level endorsement of the importance of corporate C&E would be a good first step toward articulating a coherent policy. For example, in the Department of Justice (DOJ), while the Attorney General has come close to this in endorsing the Organisation for Economic Co-operation and Development (OECD) Working Group on Bribery's issuance of the *Good Practice Guidance on Internal Controls, Ethics and Compliance*, there ideally should be a broader endorsement that applies in all areas of enforcement.

The need for such a high-level approach is particularly clear in the DOJ. While the department appears to set out a clear policy favoring strong C&E programs in the *U.S. Attorneys' Manual*, one division within DOJ has been allowed to completely ignore the manual, effectively thwarting this policy. The Antitrust Division refers cavalierly to any C&E program that is not perfect as being a "failed program," which gets no benefit or recognition from the division. The Antitrust Division is so opposed to compliance programs that it has even failed to include them as a condition for companies' participation in its leniency program. Little wonder, then, that managers in the corporate world look with skepticism at government pronouncements on compliance programs, when an entire division at DOJ sends the message that they are unimportant.

Endorsement of strong C&E programs should not stop at the executive branch. The legislature needs to step up to the plate as well. It should be expressed legislatively that the first goal of law enforcement and regulation is to protect the public from harm and not just to collect fines after the public has been hurt. The legislature should recognize the power of prevention and, by extension, the social value of companies conducting self-policing. This should be articulated as an important public policy goal, to be considered by agencies when issuing rules, enforcement agencies when pursuing violations, and courts in applying the laws.

Tie the Policy to Enforcement Decisions in a Meaningful Way

To bring the policy to life, it is essential that enforcement agencies take C&E programs into account in their enforcement decisionmaking. DOJ (except for the Antitrust Division) has taken a good first step in this regard by stating this as policy in the *U.S. Attorneys' Manual*. It is best if the policy makes it clear that there are many ways that a C&E program can affect the government's enforcement approach. These include determining:

1. whether to proceed against a company at all
2. whether to prosecute criminally or civilly
3. what charges to bring
4. how much of a penalty to pursue
5. whether to charge individuals rather than the company
6. whether to pursue a subsidiary instead of a parent

7. whether and to what extent to seek additional relief, such as monitoring and an imposed compliance program obligation.

Through this kind of approach, government helps to make clear that a company's diligence in preventing and detecting wrongdoing goes to the heart of organizational culpability and is not just a nice add-on corporate decoration.

Show Through the Enforcement Process That C&E Really Does Matter

In the Criminal Division of DOJ, it is already the stated policy to consider C&E programs in enforcement decisions, but there has been precious little evidence to demonstrate that this is ever done in practice. This leads to an important point: Policies do not matter unless they are acted upon. Just as a company C&E program that consists of a code of conduct and nothing more would have little if any value, so too a government policy that sits on the shelf but is ignored in practice has no real value. Once the government has articulated the right policies, the next indispensable step is to apply those policies to actual cases, and to do so in a highly visible way.

In taking a public approach to dealing with C&E programs, enforcers will be teaching as well. The private sector will watch carefully what benefits companies actually get from having C&E programs and what factors in those programs really count in decisions about enforcement.

An example of how not to build C&E into enforcement can be seen in cases where the government simply provides an undifferentiated list of factors that supposedly contributed to an enforcement decision. Then, when the government goes on to provide detail about how a company cooperated but provides no detail on that company's C&E program, the message conveyed is that what really matters to the government is the cooperation, and that the rest of the list of factors is mostly fluff. So, if a C&E program specifically results in a penalty being reduced by x percent, or results in the company only being pursued civilly, spotlighting that level of detail becomes far more attention-getting and influential in driving behavior.

It is also important for government to use these cases to educate companies on which C&E program elements matter and which do not. Thus, if the government were to say that a company's C&E program received no credit in an enforcement decision, because that program was just a code and led by a junior-level lawyer with the make-believe title of "compliance officer," that would send a powerful message to companies. On the other hand, when a company receives a complete pass in an enforcement review and is then praised for the effectiveness of its C&E program in setting internal incentives, and for having an independent and empowered CECO at the executive level, this message too will travel rapidly to other firms.

In this area, then, what government ought to do is show clearly that prior-existing C&E programs that are powered up really do matter—that they play a specific role in enforcement decisions and that this role is independent of what the company does to enhance its C&E program after the fact of a crisis or how much it cooperated in a crisis-related investigation.[3]

In April 2012, DOJ showed in a Foreign and Corrupt Practices Act (FCPA) case how this can be done. In a case involving Morgan Stanley, the department declined to proceed against the company, determining instead that an individual offender was the appropriate target for enforcement. DOJ stated that the individual acted despite the company's "efforts to maintain adequate controls designed to prevent corruption." In its press release the department noted what this meant in detail:

> Morgan Stanley maintained a system of internal controls meant to ensure accountability for its assets and to prevent employees from offering, promising or paying anything of value to foreign government officials. Morgan Stanley's internal policies, which were updated regularly to reflect regulatory developments and specific risks, prohibited bribery and addressed corruption risks associated with the giving of gifts, business entertainment, travel, lodging, meals, charitable contributions and employment. Morgan Stanley frequently trained its employees on its internal policies, the FCPA and other anti-corruption laws. Between 2002 and 2008, Morgan Stanley trained various groups of Asia-based personnel on anti-corruption policies 54 times. During the same period, Morgan Stanley trained Peterson on the FCPA seven times and reminded him to comply with the FCPA at least 35 times. Morgan Stanley's compliance personnel regularly monitored transactions, randomly audited particular employees, transactions and business units, and tested to identify illicit payments. Moreover, Morgan Stanley conducted extensive due diligence on all new business partners and imposed stringent controls on payments made to business partners.

Here, DOJ did two things that are of central importance. First, it was very clear that the existence of a diligent program played a central role in the decision not to prosecute. Second, the details of the program mattered, and the department shared these details with others.[4]

Focus on What's Real and Important in C&E Programs

Human nature being what it is, and humans liking easy answers, there are doubtless those who would like the government to provide a simple checklist of five easy steps on C&E (e.g., issue a code, have a lawyer lecture once for employees, have the CEO give a mighty and righteous speech), thereby entitling a company to a permanent get-out-of-jail-free card for having carried out those steps. But this would be a disaster for all involved. In the long term, the interest of both government and companies is better served by having government conduct only credible and insightful assessments of C&E programs.

---

3 The DOJ Criminal Division could particularly benefit from breaking with its past practice in this regard.

4 Department of Justice, Office of Public Affairs (April 25, 2012), "Former Morgan Stanley Managing Director Pleads Guilty for Role in Evading Internal Controls Required by FCPA," press release, http://www.justice.gov/opa/pr/2012/April/12-crm-534.html.

When government provides benefits to companies with diligent C&E programs, those companies and programs need to be demonstrably diligent. The government, in making this determination, must itself have credibility, so that companies know that their commitment to C&E performance has to be a serious one. If companies think they can pull the wool over the government's eyes, then C&E programs will die of starvation.

To be credible in this way, the government needs to have access to appropriate expertise sufficient to conduct a valid C&E program assessment. Such assessment needs to focus on C&E program elements that matter, and not on merely formalistic things like codes and training lectures.[5] Agencies may be well advised to develop a cadre of internal experts with the experience and knowledge to help in this task. Outside experts in the C&E field could also help government on this.

One of the best examples of core C&E program elements is the existence of a CECO who is empowered, independent, sufficiently resourced, and connected to executive power. The role of the CECO is a prime indicator of program rigor, because without powerful leadership and expertise for the program, the program is seriously weakened.[6] The following is an example of a CECO checklist that would be relatively easy for government to assess. Similar checklists could be developed for other aspects of the C&E program as well:

1. Is the CECO an executive officer (not subordinate to another officer, such as the chief financial officer or general counsel)?
2. Do the CECO's written reports reach the board without anyone else censoring or filtering them?
3. Does the CECO meet regularly with an independent committee of the board in executive session and have unfiltered access on an ad hoc basis?
4. Can the CECO only be removed by the board, not by management?
5. Is the CECO a participant in important senior management meetings (not just those specifically dealing with compliance)?
6. Does the C&E program have adequate staff and resources, including its own independent budget for which the CECO is responsible?
7. Does the CECO have autonomy, or is the title just tacked onto another officer's title (e.g., general counsel or vice president of human resources)?

---

5 Although government competence in assessing the quality of C&E programs is a key element in structuring related incentives to firms, it is also important that the burden of proof in demonstrating program quality always remains with the company. If the burden of proof somehow shifts to government to show that particular C&E programs are not effective, then that burden will likely be almost hopeless to overcome. This could result in a backlash against the whole process of considering and crediting programs

6 See the discussion in Greenberg (2009).

8. Is the CECO a C&E professional (e.g., a member of a C&E professional organization), or does he or she have other professional qualifications, such as certification or training?
9. Do other C&E professionals throughout the company have a reporting relationship to the CECO, and does the CECO have a say over their evaluations and removal?
10. Is the CECO supported by a high-level interdepartmental C&E committee?

To the extent that government can operate with this level of knowledge and insight, it will convey to companies that the focus on quality C&E programs is a serious priority. In turn, that will motivate companies to know at least as much about good C&E practice as the enforcers do, and to have a C&E program that will satisfy demanding but fair standards.

Send a Single, Coherent Message on C&E

Finally, there is a need for government to speak with one clear and coherent voice on C&E issues. Those in government who are responsible for this message need to know the field well and keep current on its developments. They should be active participants, taking every opportunity to learn.

Government should also take the next step and apply these C&E lessons to its own operations. Because government agencies are composed of human beings, they too have a need for effective C&E programs. They should be among the leaders in implementing such programs. At the U.S. federal level, the Federal Bureau of Investigation provides a good model and shows how this can be done.[7]

Among the agencies concerned with private-sector C&E programs and enforcement, there should be a strong effort to coordinate enforcement approaches. While the degree of emphasis on different C&E program elements will vary according to the specific risk area, the core elements will be the same, following the pattern established by the Federal Sentencing Guidelines. Perhaps an interagency task force or coordinating body could help with this task.

Finally, related harmonization efforts should also be pursued on an international basis. Here, again, there are models. Just as the Criminal Division of DOJ provided the best early model in the policy set forth in the *U.S. Attorneys' Manual*, so too that same division, along with the SEC, set the mark for others in its work with the OECD Working Group on Bribery. In 2010, the working group issued the first-ever multinational compliance program guidance. The Criminal Division and the SEC led the way.

Unfortunately, just as the Antitrust Division has ignored the Federal Sentencing Guidelines policy and the *U.S. Attorneys' Manual*, it has also set the wrong tone at OECD by doing nothing whatsoever to promote international standards that relate to the prevention of

---

7 See Rutgers Center for Government Compliance and Ethics, at http://rcgce.camlaw.rutgers.edu.

cartel conduct. Thus, again, it is clear that cabinet-level leadership is needed, both domestically and internationally, to lead the way.

Government exists to benefit the people. The interest of the people is not to ambush companies with larger and larger fines for misconduct, but instead to prevent violations in the first place. The public and the government have much to gain when companies and other organizations actively join the fight against corporate crime and wrongdoing. To get to this point, we need one strong policy, holding companies that fail to join the fight strictly accountable for their crimes. But to be fair and to encourage self-policing, government must make clear that those who join the fight are welcomed and will see the benefit of their good-faith efforts.